THE FLYING TIGER

McGILL-QUEEN'S NATIVE AND NORTHERN SERIES
BRUCE G. TRIGGER, EDITOR

THE

FLYING

TIGER

Women Shamans
and Storytellers of the Amur

KIRA VAN DEUSEN

McGill-Queen's University Press
Montreal & Kingston • London • Ithaca

© McGill-Queen's University Press 2001
ISBN 0-7735-2155-0 (cloth)
ISBN 0-7735-2156-9 (paper)

Legal deposit first quarter 2001
Bibliothèque nationale du Québec

Printed in Canada on acid-free paper

McGill-Queen's University Press acknowledges the financial support
of the Government of Canada through the Book Publishing Industry
Development Program (BPIDP) for its activities. It also acknowledges the
support of the Canada Council for the Arts for its publishing program.

Canadian Cataloguing in Publication Data

Van Deusen, Kira 1946–
   The Flying Tiger : women shamans and storytellers of the amur

(McGill-Queen's native and northern series ; 25)
Includes bibliographical references and index.
ISBN 0-7735-2155-0 (cloth)
ISBN 0-7735-2156-9 (paper)   *TOC*

   1. Women shamans–Russia (Federation)–Amur–Folklore.
2. Tunguses–Folklore. 3. Legends–Russia (Federation)–
Amur. 4. Tales–Russia (Federation)–Amur. I. Title. II. Series

GR345.V35 2001   398.2'089'9410577   C00-901039-4

This book was designed by David LeBlanc and typeset in 10.5/12.5
New Baskerville

CONTENTS

Introduction: Shamanic Storytelling of the Amur Region

The Flying Tiger is a collection of more than fifty legends, magic tales, and life stories told to me by indigenous storytellers of the Udegei, Nanai, Ul'chi, and Nivkh people of the Russian Far East in 1993–97.[1] As a storyteller, I had begun reading and telling Siberian folk tales and became curious to learn more about them at first hand. I was fortunate in making contact with Nadezhda Kimonko in Khabarovsk, who made my travel through the villages of the Amur region possible. Many of these stories have never been published before in any language and in giving their permission the tellers seemed delighted with the idea that their tales would be heard in other countries, hoping this might lead to cultural exchange as well as the preservation of their ancient sacred stories. In accordance with their wishes I have tried to set the stories in context, rather than analyzing them in folkloristic terms.

Stories like the ones in this collection are the best source of information about Siberian shamanism. Oral storytelling is the way shamans themselves convey spiritual truth. The images and plots of magic tales and legends recount the whole course of a shaman's life and work, from the call and initiation, through relationships with helping spirits, to healing the sick through recovery of stolen souls, and accompanying the souls of the dead to the next world. Magic tales and legends preserved in oral tradition are records of shamanic history, philosophy, and art – showing us new ways of looking at the world. But they are also important to shamanic practice in another way – through the power of words and sounds, stories and songs act directly on the listener to bring about healing and spiritual growth. More important than the content of the tales is the process of telling them – the ways a storyteller chooses the tale, the details added or removed, the tone – all of these make storytelling a spiritual act. Stories and songs are not objects or artifacts but living beings.

Most of the stories in this collection were told by women. In the Amur region, the majority of traditional storytellers are women, a reflection of their long history as carriers of oral tradition. In the Amur region, unlike many parts of Siberia, women told epics as well as shorter stories. My sense is that the way men use stories in this culture is different – men told traditional tales mostly while hunting, while women's tales were told in the home. The men's traditions have changed more radically than the women's during the twentieth century because of their changed lifestyle under communism.

My background for this work includes an undergraduate degree in Russian language and literature, training in folklore and ethnography, and several years as a professional storyteller, which influenced both what I looked for and what I heard. I am familiar with the ways audience interacts with teller, the way images form on the inner eye and are transmitted from one person to a group, or even to a single listener. I am particularly drawn to tales that I would like to add to my repertoire. But long before I began to tell traditional tales in front of consciously gathered audiences, I had been aware of the function of "kitchen-table" storytelling in my own life. Friends would gather and we would tell over the events of our inner and outer lives – a process that helped us to make sense of things and to maintain a sense of humour in the face of difficulties. Now I have learned that the kitchen table holds the same place in the cultures of women on the other side of the world.

When I came to the Amur region, I wanted to find out if the stories people told were the same as the ones I had read in books. After all, reading stories is not the same as knowing what stories people tell, and what makes them laugh and cry. I learned that there was a wealth of stories that had not been published, representing a complex philosophy and a way of looking at the world that is full of wisdom and humour. There were stories that told difficult truths about family relations and the political processes of colonization, as well as those told for a good laugh.

In order to understand the stories I sometimes needed to break through the boundaries of my own cultural background and its expectations, learning to see with new eyes. Early in my travels I dreamed that a friend gave me an odd new pair of glasses. The lenses were very thick and bulged out in the middle like old-fashioned electric fuses. "These will help you to understand what you see," my friend said. This was strange, since through the glasses everything looked completely blurry. But since then the stories themselves have come to act as my new glasses. The picture has cleared, helping me to cross the boundaries between cultures and between the worlds of spirit and of everyday reality.

Often the best storytellers are shamans, who are well acquainted with crossing those boundaries and speaking of what they have seen. Most shamans claim ancestry in both human and spiritual worlds, and their first mission is to serve their people. They heal illness through spiritual journeys to other worlds, where they retrieve souls that have been shocked from the body or abducted by spirits. (Even an affectionate relative may inadvertently take a person's soul when they leave for the land of the dead.) They conduct religious ceremonies, with the participation of the whole community, and predict weather and behaviour. In the Amur region the highest function of the shaman is that of conducting the souls of the dead to *Buni*, the next world. Indigenous people assert that such journeys can literally happen.

Their tales present a complex network of shamanic imagery, conveying pictures of what shamans see and do on their journeys to other worlds. Some of the tales tell the life history of specific shamans who are still remembered. They also reflect the specific humour of the shamanic world, the interplay of jokes and very serious spiritual truth. Not all shamanic stories are intended for human listeners: this is especially clear in the case of hunting, where tales were told specifically to attract the spirits of the forest who would send game to the hunters.

Indigenous people see the shaman's path as dangerous. Even contact with a shaman can be threatening, which is why people avoid consulting them if it is not clearly necessary. The spirits are connected with death and are often far from benevolent or pleasant. While some Westerners may romanticize the shaman's path and desire to follow it, my friends have told me that the dangers involved explain why no one in a traditional society would actually choose to be a shaman – many resist the call. It is precisely because of the danger that shamans are needed – ordinary people are fully capable of dealing with benevolent spirits themselves.

Before the Soviet period there were many shamans, both women and men. Under Stalin and his successors this ancient form of healing and religious thought was severely persecuted and many shamans died in the gulags. Today there are very few left, and the younger people consult them to learn about their traditions and to see how they can help solve the desperate problems facing communities today – economic development, gaining control over the land, cultural revival, alcoholism treatment. This is a very important time of transformation on both personal and social levels, and the old stories take on new meaning as the old social order crumbles.[2]

The storytellers I met represent several generations, their lives spanning most of the twentieth century. During this time the people of the Amur region have moved from older traditional lifestyles that included fishing and nomadic hunting in the taiga forest to collectivized village life under the communist system. During the Soviet period storytelling was discouraged along with the use of native languages. Now, in the post-Soviet period, people are negotiating another series of changes as they cope with economic problems at the same time they try to revive their cultural traditions.

The storytellers spoke a number of languages. The older generation tended to be most comfortable in their native language, Udegei, Nanai, Ul'chi, or Nivkh. They translated their tales into Russian for me themselves, or called on friends and relatives to translate. (All of these languages except Nivkh (an isolate) are members of the Tungus-Manchu branch of the Altai family.) The middle generation (45–65) is usually fully bilingual in the native language and Russian, while the younger generations speak only Russian. Most of the stories were told in homes, where I recorded them on tape. Most of the elder shamans and tellers have died since I recorded them in the early 1990s. The translations from Russian to English are my own, and I have conveyed the voices of the original tellers as closely as possible in the medium of another language.

I have used the Library of Congress system of transliterating the Cyrillic alphabet. Exceptions to this are some familiar names such as Alexander, and a few Nanai words where I strove to make the pronunciation unmistakable. The apostrophe in words like "Ul'chi" does not represent a sound but serves to soften the preceding consonant.

Most of the stories fall into the categories of *nimanku* or *telungu*, as they are called in Tungus languages. *Nimanku* refers to the "magic tale" (or "wonder tale") and shares a linguistic root with words referring to shamanic ritual and the concept of seeing clairvoyantly, while *telungu* derives from the word meaning "to tell or relate" and thus corresponds more closely with the legend. It is not so much the kinds of story events that distinguish the genres but the way in which the teller has come to know them and the purpose of telling them.

Women's shamanic and storytelling traditions differ from those of men in several ways. As in many cultures, women were mainly oriented toward home and family. One fascinating aspect of the women's story tradition is its connection with their magnificent embroidery, which acted as a spiritual force of protection and reflects many of the same images found in story. Women were less showy and obvious than men when acting as shamans, which is one reason they were less persecuted than male shamans under Stalin and have survived to the present.

Some important shamanic themes in Amur women's traditions are found in tales of a girl who lives alone, completely competent and independent, until some challenge propels her into an initiatory adventure. Also fascinating are tales of the sacred nature of twins, of death and rebirth, of marriage with animals leading to the foundation of new clans by women, and the ways historical legends are being used in the present. These tales and the lives of the people telling them are a testament to a great complexity of thought and spirituality and the ways it facilitates change in the post-Soviet world.

Acknowledgments

I am grateful to many friends who have helped me with their suggestions and encouragement. At all stages of my work Bruce Grant has shared his extensive knowledge as well as his network of resources and his sense of humour. Marjorie Mandelstam Balzer also gave many helpful suggestions, as did Mike Ballantyne, Liz Fitch, Murray Shoolbraid, David and Andrea Spalding, and the people no author can do without – my writing group: Sally Stiles, Michael Boxall, Nancy Lee, and Carol Shaben. Professional storytellers including Anne Anderson, Mary Louise Chown, Wes Fine Day, Nan Gregory, Johanna Hiemstra, Helen O'Brian, Louise Profiet-Leblanc, Kay Stone, and many others have discussed these stories with me, offering their valuable insights. I am grateful to the organizers of the Yukon Storytelling Festival for helping me to make my initial contacts in the Amur region, and the Vancouver Storytelling

Festival for bringing Udegei storytellers to Canada in 1998. Thanks also to Leslie Conton for her friendship and insights on shamanism. I am grateful to everyone at McGill-Queens University Press for their enthusiasm and skill in producing this book. Thanks also to *Shaman: Journal of the International Society for Shamanistic Research* for permission to use my work previously published by them in 1996, vol. 4, nos. 1–2, and 1997, vol. 5, no. 2, and to Murray Pleasance for the use of several of his photographs.

But most of all, my gratitude and special thanks to Nadezhda Kimonko who worked so hard to make my travels possible, and to the storytellers, shamans, and many other people who shared their homes and lives with me in the Amur region, making my stay there such a rich and pleasurable experience.

Glossary

(Na=Nanai; Ud=Udegei; Ul=Ul'chi; Ni=Nivkh; R=Russian)

Aiolu – a small enclosed shed (Ud)
Altaic languages – a large language family which includes
   the Mongolian, Turkic, and Tungusic branches as well
   as Japanese and Korean. The Altaic family is named for
   the Altai mountains where it is believed to have originated. The Udegei, Nanai, and Ul'chi languages are
   part of the Tungusic branch.
Amba(n) evil spirit (Na, Ud, Ul)
Ana – dugout boat (Ud)
Anda – friend (Na, Ud)
Apa – an evil spirit (Na)
Arachu – a place prepared for the ceremonial killing of a
   bear (Ul)

Atoya – a box in which men keep small tools and smoking materials (Ud)

Banya – bath-house (R)

Belye – Heroine of Udegei tales (Ud)

Buni – land of the dead (Na)

Burkhan – Figures representing deities, often made of wood (R)

Chan – a large pot iron (Na)

Chongo – air space at the top of a house, under the roof. (Ul)

Dacha – a summer place where city people grow vegetables. Located anywhere from a short bus ride to a trip which takes many hours, a dacha may or may not include buildings. (R)

Duchieke – Nanai violin (Na)

Duse – the flying tiger, helping spirit of shaman Anga (Ul)

Dyuli – spirit figure (Na)

Emenda – Foolish and awkward woman in Udegei folklore. Often appears as a frog. (Ud)

Fudin (Pudi) – Heroine of Nanai and Ul'chi tales (Na, Ul)

Jiagda – wooden figures raised outdoors in honour of a person's ancestors (Ud)

Kamlanie – shaman's ceremonial activity. (from Turkic *kam*, shaman) (R)

Kanda Mafa – old man, evil figure in Udegei tales (Ud)

Kasa – Ceremony of conducting the souls of the dead to *Buni.* (Na)

Kava – traditional Udegei house, covered with bark (Ud)

Kha – fish-trap (Ud)

Khanyaunya khuni – Ceremony of conducting the dead to the next world. (Ud)

Khatka – Soft grass used to insulate footwear. (Ud)

Khure – frog (Na)

Kilaa – swan (Ul)

Kolkhoz – a collective organization for agricultural work, fishing, hunting, and other activities established by the Soviet government during the 1930s and later (R)

Kya-kya – sounds used for calling spirits (Na)

Mangbo – powerful place. Nanai and Ul'chi name for
the Amur
Mergen – hero of Nanai and Ul'chi tales
Nakan – sleeping bench (Na)
Nakusa – straps which hold skis on (Ud)
Ningma (or nimanku) – magic tale (Tungus languages)
Ola – exclamation (Na)
Omorochka – plank or dugout boat (R)
Podya – spirit of place (Na, Ud, Ul)
Sagdi-mama – female deity who brings and protects life of
children (Ud)
Salome – a dish made of berries mixed with dried fish
(Ud)
Sevén – Spirit-figures, usually belonging to shamans
(Na, Ul, Ud)
Sheat-fish (Russian *som*) a large freshwater catfish, *Silurus
glanis*, native to Eurasia.
Taiga – temperate forest (R from Turkic)
Taimen – a large fish of the salmon family. Can grow as
large as 1.5 m, weighing 60 kg.
Tapchan – bed (Na)
Telungu – Legend (Tungus languages)
Tudin – person similar to shaman who diagnoses illness
and acts as control on shaman's trance. (Na)
Tungus – a branch of the Altai language family. The
northern Tungus languages include Even and Evenk,
while the southern Tungus include Nanai, Udegei,
Ul'chi, Negidal, Manchu, Sibu, and Solon. Before the
Soviet period the name Tungus was applied specifically
to the people now called Evenk.
Turkic – a large branch of the Altai language family which
includes Turkish, Azerbaijani, Kazakh, Kirgiz, Bashkir,
Turkmen, Tatar, Uzbek, Tuvan, Altai, Khakass, Uighur,
Dolgan, Sakha (Yakut), and others.
Uli – traditional footwear (Ud)
Unuchku – Nanai shaman's drum
Utya – toad (Ud)

Vagda – the constellation the Pleiades (Ud)

Verst – a measure of distance used in tsarist Russia, equal to 1.06 km.

Yampa – Shaman's belt with bells. Often has the form of a snake. (Ud, Na)

Yegdyga – hero of Udegei tales. (Ud)

Ypila – a shaman's conversation with spirits, asking forgiveness (Na)

Yukola – dried fish (R)

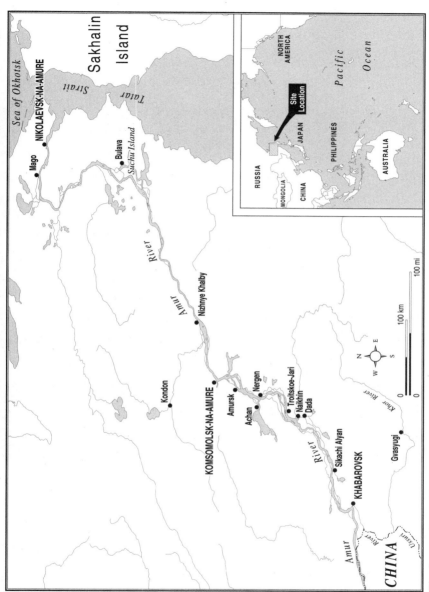

The Lower Amur River

Two Nivkh women playing musical instruments made of a reed.
Poronaisk, Sakhalin Island. (Photo by Murray Pleasance.)

THE FLYING TIGER

"When I was a young girl, I married a tiger. My tiger
babies became my helping spirits. They fly me to
other worlds."

1

Udegei Storytellers in Gvasyugi

Nadezhda Kimonko and I met in the town of Poronaisk on Sakhalin Island in the fall of 1992. We were both shivering in a cold corridor at a festival on folk arts of the "Peoples of the North," as the indigenous peoples of the Russian Far East were called at the time.[1] Nadia was representing an arts group from the city of Khabarovsk. I was representing Canada, playing fiddle tunes and translating for six other Canadians. I was also pursuing my own interest – looking for storytellers. We had been invited to Poronaisk by the ensemble Mengume Ilga who had performed at the Yukon International Storytelling Festival earlier that year, giving Canadians a glimpse of what seemed like another world.

Nadia took me aside and began asking questions. "What problems do Native people face in Canada today?" She was amazed to hear about land claims, alcoholism, unemployment, suicide and isolation. "Our people have just the same problems," she said, "but we didn't know it was like that in Canada!" Then we talked about logging. I told her about the west coast of Vancouver Island where I lived, the rapidly diminishing old growth forests, clearcut logging, decreasing numbers of salmon, polluted water. And she told me about her people – the Udegei.

The Udegei were traditionally a hunting people. They live far from cities in the taiga north of Vladivostok, in the same realm as the Siberian tiger. Their numbers are small, about 2,000, one-third of whom still speak the Udegei language.

"We are forest people," said Nadia, "our needs are simple." Before Soviet times they lived in small family groups in the taiga forest and have since come to live in three villages, created by the communist administration. "But our hearts are still in the great forests – hunting, fishing, trapping fur-bearing animals and digging ginseng." Simple needs easily met – provided the taiga remains intact.

Following *perestroika* the government granted logging rights to Hyundai, who came in with the latest equipment. They could clearcut 1,400 acres a day. At that rate it wouldn't take long for the hunting, fishing, and ginseng to disappear for the Udegei and the tigers. "Korean workers poison the rivers, poach, and recognize no laws – and the local administration can do nothing to stop them (Vakhtin 1994:64.)"

"People have gone to talk to Yeltsin," said Nadia, "but it doesn't make any difference. What can be done?"

Her intensity moved me. She wasn't used to big business. This was her first experience of large-scale western capitalism, and she experienced the full outrage of it, unlike veterans of other environmental battles who might sigh and say, "Oh no, not another one," before getting outraged. (As years passed and I got to know Nadia better I also found she was not yet numb to violence on television.) I promised to see what I could do. Nadia gave me an address in Khabarovsk and then another one, much shorter, which she said was her permanent home, in the village of Gvasyugi.

4

Floating bridge at the village of Gvasyugi.

Back home I wrote to Greenpeace and Audubon, who already knew about the logging and were working actively on it. I wrote to Nadia in Gvasyugi, which was not on the map, and she wrote back from the city of Khabarovsk. There was important work to be done in the city, she said. Most Udegei literally can't stand urban living so the work of organizing cultural activities on a large scale had fallen to Nadia, who has a greater tolerance. Thanks for caring about the logging, she said. Why didn't I come and visit the Khabarovsk Territory? Could she help me find storytellers? I asked in return. Lots of storytellers, she replied. Storytellers, shamans, elders who remember the old ways of life.

A year later, in September 1993, I landed at Khabarovsk. A lot had changed – there was a brand new airport building with the music of Paul Simon playing, and people were better dressed. But the warm welcome was the same.

The next day we drove out of Khabarovsk past hundreds of city dweller's dachas and gardens. First we went along a major highway, by which I mean it was paved, then down a highway that was not paved but still had a fair amount of traffic and led to a couple of villages with rather decrepit-looking sawmills. I thought about Hyundai.

Then we started to meander down a road that seemed to be very little travelled. It rose gently into the hills and the trees got denser. Although they looked familiar, almost none of the trees here were exactly like the trees where I live, almost due east across the ocean, on a small island off the west coast of Canada. The willows were not our willows, the pines and cedars were not ours. There were no firs or arbutus. But there was an incredible wealth of unfamiliar plant life, trees, vines, ferns, berries. Even from the car window I could see that it would be a good place to be a hunter-gatherer. We saw a mink, a roe-deer, an owl and little birds with yellow bellies that bobbed as they flew.

We arrived at the village and I was relieved to see that it was beautiful. Many cities and villages I had visited in Russia were ugly and depressing, with large concrete apartment buildings, broken iron fences, and heating plants belching coal smoke. Here small wooden houses were scattered along a small river and each garden was bursting with fall flowers.

We walked across a footbridge made of planks floating on logs and I began to meet people, most of them related to Nadia. They were all very busy, getting in their potatoes, fishing, and helping other people get ready to go fishing. These are the basic autumn activities in the Amur region, especially since the breakdown of the Soviet Union. People are now finding their own food supplies, since it's quite likely there won't be anything coming from outside, and anything that might come will be too expensive.

We moved in with Nadia's Aunt Tosia, whose house seemed to be the central hub of information and activity in Gvasyugi. Life centred around the summer kitchen, a tiny building with a gas stove, small table, chairs, and lace curtains. Sitting at the table for a couple of hours we drank tea, ate delicious fish soup with potatoes and fresh pancakes with local honey, and got totally up-to-date on what was happening in this village of three hundred. People stopped in and left messages about what the kids were doing after school. They delivered fish and picked up honey. And they exchanged news. It was just like my memories of kitchen tables in rural Canada in the mid-seventies.

Some of the village's young people had moved away and others were scandalously drunk, shouting in the streets. Electricity was produced by a noisy diesel station in the centre of the village. It came on for the school in the daytime and for the houses in the evening, in time for everyone to watch the Mexican TV soap opera "Simply Maria," which obsessed all of Russia in the earlier years of perestroika. But sometimes there was no power at the school in the daytime and Tosia, who went in to cook lunch for the children, complained bitterly. The day I visited the school I was almost glad the power was off because the darkness of the hallways hid my tears when I looked at rooms with no books and a chemistry lab that held three desks and two empty beakers.

People in Tosia's kitchen were trying to understand what must be done to get the hunting rights for the land around Gvasyugi into Udegei hands. Up until now it had seemed unnecessary to do anything – there was plenty of room, plenty of animals, plenty of trees. Now, more and more often, people from the city were bringing rich hunters, sometimes foreigners, who were shooting all the fur-bearing animals. They took them away to make money that never came back. Poaching further depleted the stocks of animals. And there was the experience of Krasnyi Yar, the other Udegei village south of here, the one invaded by Hyundai. Forests were receding rapidly. Tosia and her cousin Valentina were working on that. They were determined, intelligent, and energetic, but they battled an information blackout to the villages. There is not so much as a telephone in Gvasyugi and mail service is unreliable. Nadia brought the latest news from Khabarovsk and there was a lively discussion.

But the big news in the kitchen that first day was that a man had disappeared on the river, presumed drowned. He must have been drunk and fallen from his boat. Although nobody seemed to have liked the man much, women began mobilizing to help the family. Tosia's husband had also drowned while fishing. These waters are treacherous even to those with years of experience on them. People did not dwell on tragedy but started preparing food.

Nadia and I left to go looking for storytellers, which meant sitting in other people's kitchens, drinking more tea and eating more pancakes with honey. The first person we visited was Eofu Sisilievich Kimonko, fondly known as Grandpa Kostya. That first day we sat in the darkening late afternoon and chatted. He didn't remember any stories, he said, but he told about building the little bark-covered hut called a *kava* out by the river. This is the kind of house the Udegei built when they lived nomadically before the Soviet period. Children played in it now. Small and easily constructed at each new living place, the *kava* had a framework of sticks covered with wide strips of willow bark. There was a hole in the roof for the smoke and a hook hanging from the rafter for the cooking pot. Although the Udegei might return annually to the same seasonal living-places, the building materials would not last long, and so the houses were constructed anew with each season. This meant they were always fresh and clean. In summer the willow bark helped keep mosquitoes away, and in the winter people dug the ground out underneath to prevent drafts in their sleeping places and to keep the house warmer. The Udegei also made their own dugout canoes and dogsleds and used them to move from one place to another along the rivers.

Grandpa Kostya took a lot of pleasure in telling us how rich men used to have more than one wife. Sometimes if an older brother died, the younger brother would marry his wife. Sometimes young men bought their wives. Kostya's mother-in-law used to joke that she had cost thirty-five

8

tsarist rubles. The men didn't always pay though. Did they steal their wives? "Why no," Kostya cackled, "we didn't steal them, we took them!"

When men went hunting they first made sacrifices of flour and cakes to the trees and to the spirits of their amulets. Kostya taught young men how to carry out this ritual. He recalled one place, far away in the woods up a mountain, where there was a little house with a portrait of a Chinese man. They used to make sacrifices there too, he said, without understanding why the Chinese portrait was there, simply because it was a sacred place.

It got dark and we went home. But the next day Kostya remembered a story after all. He put on his embroidered green velvet coat and sat in the *kava* to tell it to us, first in the Udegei language and then in Russian.

TWO GIRLS AND KANDA MAFA

This happened in the winter. Two girls were living alone. One day the younger sister went out for firewood and the older one was at home embroidering.

Kanda Mafa, the cannibal god, came in and said, "Hello! Now, girl, you look for the lice on my head." She gathered and smashed them. Then he said, "Now I'll look on your head."

"All right," she said.

"Here, I'll put them in your mouth and you crush them with your teeth."

She stuck her tongue out and he reached in and tore it out. She died.

He went out and put her tongue in the barn. Then he went away.

The younger sister came back with a full sled of firewood. She was coming up over the steep bank and called her sister for help. When there was no answer she went

9

looking and found the older girl sitting there dead, with no tongue.

The younger sister searched and searched and finally found that tongue in the barn. She put the tongue back in and her sister came to life.

The older sister told how Kanda Mafa had come.

"He'll be back," she said. "Let's watch out for him, and when he comes we'll hit him over the head and then run away."

They hid.

Kanda Mafa came back.

The sisters put the old man to sleep by searching for the lice on his head. The old man fell asleep. They hit him over the head with a hammer.

He lost consciousness and they ran away. They came to the river. There was ice on the water, but some open areas between. A man was there – the hunter Yegdyga. He put his pole over the water and helped the girls to get across.

Kanda Mafa came running, with his head wrapped up in a rag. He ran back and forth along the bank.

"Help me!" he called to Yegdyga. "I want to get that girl and eat her up!"

Yegdyga put his pole out, but when Kanda Mafa was halfway across he pulled the pole away and dropped the evil old man into the water. The river carried him away.

Yegdyga married the two girls. ▼

I had never heard stories like this before. I found them as surprising as Nadia found the idea of people watching murders on TV for entertainment. I later learned that the hair is the site of one form of human lifeforce and that playing with the hair, or picking out lice, is a way of gaining control over a person's soul. And I thought about the implications of losing one's tongue, and with it the ability to speak – the experience of women who married into clans speaking a different dialect. But for now I was simply amazed to hear such things spoken of in such a matter-of-fact way. In the coming days I heard many more such tales in which these themes and others were repeated and embroidered with variations as creative as the designs on Kostya's coat.

From Kostya's we rambled on to sit in the kitchen with Valentina Tunsyanovna Kyalundzyuga, storyteller, teacher, dancer, folklore collector, and political activist. She was a slender woman in her mid-fifties, quick in her movements and quick to laugh. It is easy to talk about the many things she does, from running the village council, to writing books, to raising three children and a number of grand-children – but the other part of the story is the straightfor-ward good humour and energy with which she does them. Like Kostya, she had a sparkle in her eye. Her house was surrounded by a big garden gone somewhat to seed. Be-sides vegetables and flowers, Valentina had transplanted healing plants from the taiga so that they would be conven-ient when she needed them.

Valentina told many of my favourite stories, like this one about that same Kanda Mafa. He is sometimes called the can-nibal god (Mafa means bear, Kanda is the old man) and his wife is known as the goddess of the earth. He appears in many Udegei tales, as do the hero Yegdyga, or marksman, and the heroine-artist Belye, and the awkward and lazy Emenda.

KANDA MAFA AND THE BONES

A girl lived with her brother. The brother was always hunt-ing and bringing back fish and meat. She prepared skins and made clothes, boots, and food.

One morning the sister woke up, took her drum, and began to sing. She must have had some sort of dream. She said to her brother, "You will go out. On the way you'll find a dead owl. Take it with you. Farther along you'll find a dead rabbit. Take that too. And go on. You'll hear some people. Hide and listen to find out who is going by. Then you'll see how to act."

And so she played her drum and told her brother Yegdyga what she had seen. He got ready and set out. Before he left she gave him half of her comb and half of her sharpening stone, and he put them in his hunting bag. True, on the way he found a dead owl. He took it in his bag and went on. And then he found the dead rabbit, put it in his bag and went on.

It was quiet in the taiga. Suddenly he heard someone driving, making this sound: chok chok chok chok! He got up into a tree that was bending down and looked to see who would appear. He saw Kanda Mafa with his old woman sitting on a sleigh pulled by wild boars. They were driving along, chok chok chok chok chok. They went by and didn't notice Yegdyga.

Then he waited and heard someone else coming. It was Emenda, the older sister. Female wild boars were pulling her. She went by.

He thought he could come down now but then ... He could barely see her, she was all bent over. She could just barely pull the sleigh, she had no dogs or anything. He sat and looked. It was Belye, the younger daughter pulling the sleigh. She went by without looking. She was just pulling the sleigh, all tired and bent over. She looked up and thought, "What is that, an owl or a rabbit?" But she went on.

He looked at the sleigh – it was full of bones. Why bones?

He jumped down from the tree, took his stick and hooked onto the end of the sleigh so that it stopped. She pulled and pulled and couldn't move it. He was holding on to the sleigh. She turned around, saying, "What's going on here? What is it caught on? Why can't I move this sleigh?"

She looked back and saw Yegdyga there holding on to his stick, holding the sleigh. He threw the bones out.

"What are these bones for?" he asked.

"My parents eat human meat," she said. "If they don't find anyone, they make soup from the bones."

"I want to come with you," he said.

"You can't," she said, "They'll kill you."

"We'll see about that," he said.

So they went on.

They stopped for the night. They made a hut of fir branches and got a fire going. Belye didn't come close to the others but made her camp far away.

Then Emenda came running – per, per, per, per went her little feet. She was all ragged and uncombed. She saw Yegdyga and her face changed; she turned red, she turned white!

She ran home and called to her parents, "Mother, father, Yegdyga is there with Belye and he's so good looking! He's big and healthy. Now we'll have a feast!"

They were glad there would be something to eat.

"I'll wait," said Kanda Mafa. "Let him lie down to sleep."

Then Emenda came and said "Let's boil up some of those bones." She put on the pot and boiled water, then put in the bones to make broth.

Belye and Yegdyga sat by the fire and he asked her, "How do they kill?"

"Like this. When we lie down to sleep he'll ask me where you are and then kill you with a spear."

Then Emenda came and took away the pot with the bones, and they lay down. Belye lay down and put the dead owl next to her and Yegdyga lay at her feet.

Late that night Kanda Mafa came and called out "Chikhya, Chikhya,[2] where is Yegdyga?"

Belye replied, "Next to me, next to me."

He struck with his spear, heard the crunching of bones, and saw blood. Yegdyga moaned as if he were dying. Of course the old man had hit the owl, but he didn't know that. He went away well satisfied.

In the morning Emenda came running, looking for meat, getting ready for breakfast. She saw Yegdyga sitting there smoking his pipe. She turned red, she turned white! She didn't say anything but ran back to her parents and said, "Father, father, he is alive, sitting there by the fire smoking his pipe!"

"Never mind, tonight we will kill him."

Night came and again Yegdyga asked, "How will they kill?"

"This time he will come with a heated spear."

He lay next to her and they put the dead rabbit at her feet. In the night Kanda Mafa came and asked "Where is Yegdyga?"

"He's at my feet."

So he stuck the spear in and there was a smell of cooking meat. He heard the sound of bones breaking.

Yegdyga lay there under the blanket moaning in a dying voice. Kanda Mafa went away well satisfied and in the morning Emenda came looking for breakfast. Again there was Yegdyga, sitting by the fire smoking his pipe.

Again she ran back to her parents. "He's still alive!" she wailed.

"How can that be?" said Kanda Mafa. "I heard the bones break, I smelled the meat cooking. He must be a great shaman. But today I will kill him before my own eyes. Kanda Mafa is also a great shaman."

"What will they do today?" Yegdyga asked Belye.

"Today they will invite you to eat and they'll serve you poisoned food."

They made *salome*, a dish made of berries mixed with dried fish – and they added poison. Emenda came and invited him. He took a hollow reed and put it down his shirt.

Kanda Mafa said, "Sit close to me. We'll celebrate!" And he gave Yegdyga food.

Yegdyga pretended to eat but really he put all the food down the reed under his shirt. Meanwhile Emenda was hungry and sneaked some of his food. She fell down, unconscious.

"What is the matter with her?" asked Yegdyga.

"She's just embarrassed," said her parents, and they took her away. He took the reed out and threw the poisoned food into the fire. They waited for him to die, but he didn't die.

"All right," said Kanda Mafa. "Tonight we will show our shamanic power. Then he won't get away or fool us. We'll kill him for sure."

Evening came and he said, "Yegdyga, let's compete as shamans. Show me what you can do. We'll meet by the fire."

Yegdyga agreed. He made the seven wooden figures called *sevéns*,[3] and put them around the fire. Then they started to compete. Kanda Mafa went first, and then Yegdyga next. That's the way it should be, with Yegdyga last so then they would kill him. Kanda-Mafa jumped and danced around the fire and then suddenly sat down.

Udegei shamanic *sevéns* in the village museum, Gvasyugi.

"Now, it's your turn. You show us what kind of shaman you are."

They started the fire again and Yegdyga began to dance. He'd made the *sevéns* so that when the firelight shone on them it looked as if first one and then the other was laughing. They all had strange mouths and eyes. Probably Yegdyga was jumping around too. The old people started to laugh. They laughed until they fell down.

And while they were laughing, Yegdyga and Belye ran away. They ran and ran and ran, and by the time the old people came to, Yegdyga and Belye were far away.

Kanda Mafa and his wife started to chase after them. They ran and ran. Yegdyga and Belye looked back – the old man was ahead and the old woman was coming along behind with her hair flying.

As they ran along, Yegdyga threw out the comb his sister had given him. "Grow up into thick bushes," he said and threw it out. Behind them grew thick bushes.

They looked back and saw the old people coming along, all ragged and torn. Soon they would catch up. They were all getting tired. "What to do now? Now they'll catch up with us for sure."

Then he threw out the half sharpening stone and said, "Become big rocky mountains!" The stone turned into rocky mountains and the old people couldn't get past them. Yegdyga and Belye got back to his home and there they got married.

Kanda Mafa and his wife stayed behind the mountains. That's all! ▼

Valentina told this story and the following ones first in the Udegei language and then in Russian. She is part of the generation that is perfectly bilingual. Older people are often weak in Russian while younger people speak the adopted language almost exclusively. People in their forties through sixties speak both in varying degrees, depending on their education. Valentina collected many Udegei folk tales during the

1960s and 1970s and they have been published in a scholarly bilingual Udegei-Russian edition (Simonov 1998). She worked hard to convince the Academy of Sciences of the necessity of using four additional letters in the Cyrillic alphabet when writing the Udegei language. These letters represent sounds that do not exist in Russian but which are needed if Udegei is not to become confusing, if not incomprehensible.[4] She is concerned that the language may be lost, as are many languages of peoples whose numbers are small. The Soviet government discouraged the use of native languages, along with nearly all aspects of indigenous culture and the pressures of modernization also discourage the use of languages other than Russian.

The story of "Kanda Mafa and the Bones" contains several shamanic themes. Besides the divination done by Yegdyga's sister and the competition around the fire, there are images of death and rebirth in the bones, thought to contain one aspect of the soul. In a Siberian shaman's initiatory vision, spirits often take the novice apart bone by bone, searching for the extra bone that conveys shamanic ability. Keeping an animal's bones in their original order helps it to take on new flesh and return again to the hunters.

Yegdyga's quest to find a wife resembles a shaman's journey both in its difficulty and in the fact that the hero brings someone back to his own land. The image of magic flight, with the comb and stone creating forests and rocky cliffs, recalls the time of creation. Often in similar tales a teller will point to a specific feature of the local landscape, saying, "It turned into that rocky cliff." In a more practical sense, the search for a wife recalls the time when Udegei tradition forbade marriage within one's own clan and young men frequently travelled far away to find a bride.

There is one more level of shamanic imagery in this tale – humour. Listeners laugh at the references to death and rebirth, since the hero doesn't really die. As Kanda Mafa says, "He must be a great shaman." There is more humour in the way Yegdyga tricks the cannibals at dinner and during the competition. Humour is so important in Udegei sacred tradition that making the shaman laugh is actually part of *kamlanie*.[5]

Besides tales of the taiga Valentina also tells stories about the sea. In earlier times the Udegei Kimonko clan lived on the shore of the Sea of Japan and the Tatar Strait, while the Kyalundzyugas lived inland. Valentina has collected tales from the elders of both clans. Kimonko stories reflect the lives of sea-hunters. The first of these sea stories contains references to the volcanoes on nearby Kamchatka peninsula. Valentina explained that the cooking pots in the story come from the special hut in which the hero was born, so he is protected by his mother's birth magic while going on his quest for a wife among the seagull girls. Like many such quests, this one is reminiscent of a shamanic journey to bring back a lost soul. The story tells of the complexity of life in families where men had more than one wife, a theme I saw again and again in Amur stories.

THE SEAGULL[6]

Somewhere in the taiga on the bank of a river lived Yegdyga. He lived and went hunting. One day he thought, "I'll go and find myself a bride." He made an *omorochka* (boat) and started down the river. Suddenly a wide water appeared before him. It was the sea.

He got out on the shore and thought, "How will I get across? You can't get there in an *omorochka*. Suddenly from the other side seven girls began to sing, inviting him. "Kilae, kilae," they sang, "How will you come across? An ordinary person can't do it. A hail of rocks will fall. If the salty ocean burns, how will you come across?"

"I will come across. I'll put seven cooking pots on my head. The rocks will bounce off."

"How will you come if the sea is burning?"

18

"I'll put on ice boots."[7]

And he went across. The rocks rumbled – guangutata, guangutata – they bounced off his head. The boots melted and sputtered – chaulili, chaulili. He leapt onto the shore and ran to the place where the seven girls lived. Someone was looking out at him. It was a servant woman.

There were seven beds inside. And behind the house seven *jiagda* – places for praying to the ancestors.

He asked, "Who lives here?" and the servant woman answered, "I live here alone."

"If that is so, why do you have seven beds?"

"One I use for sleeping," she replied, "one for sewing ..." And she counted them all off. "I live alone."

"Why are there seven spirit-figures?"

"Those I don't need. You can break them."

He started to break them. And then the seagulls came flying and sang a song. "Why are you breaking those figures? You are destroying our souls."

"She told me to. She said nobody needed them. But don't be angry. You invited me and I came. I want to take you back as my wives."

"We won't go until you put the spirit-figures back together," they said. "Those are the spirits of our ancestors."

So he did. He put them together and the girls agreed to come across the sea with him. They got ready and started off. They flew a long time and the oldest one started to cry out.

"I am dying. I am going to the place where my ancestors are."

"Don't die," says Yegdyga, "keep flying!" But she fell into the sea. Yegdyga's tears fell into the water like lead.

One by one they all fell into the sea until only the youngest sister was left. Already he could see his own shore.

"Don't die," he said. He grabbed her and threw her out on the shore. The bird fell on the sand. He rushed to start a fire and burned the sacred ledum (Labrador tea) plant.[8]

The girl came to life.

They went back to his native river and they stayed there. And he admired the beauty of the girl from the other side of the sea.

That's all! ▼

Stories like this one recall the physical processes of the creation of the earth and also the formation of human clans, with their ancestry in the spirit world of animals and birds. As in many cultures seven is a magic number. Valentina explained that shamanic poles (the *jiagda* or spirit-figures mentioned in the story) can turn into the dwelling place of evil spirits if the soul of a deceased person who has not been seen off to the next world takes up residence in one of them. In that case it is necessary to break the pole. But in this case the servant lies to Yegdyga – the poles are the girls' protectors, and not the dwelling place of evil spirits (Simonov 1998, 386–7).

Valentina sang the important conversations between Yegdyga and the gulls, as did Agdenka, the teller she learned the story from. Singing calls attention to these important places and adds a rhythmic lilt to the telling. Some things in life are too important to be simply spoken and therefore they must be sung. (Shamans sing their calls to the spirits.) Sometimes Valentina sings this entire story, as she did when she came to Canada in 1998 to perform at the Vancouver and Yukon Storytelling Festivals. The metric pattern of the songs (eight syllables per line) is common to sacred songs throughout much of Siberia, which links this form of storytelling to sacred tradition (Leisiö 1999). One explanation for the variation between sung and spoken stories lies in the fact that traditional Udegei people did not sing at night, believing that it might attract the spirits of the dead. Stories like this one, however, were told only at night (Podmaskin 1991, 56, 59) Since Valentina was performing outside the traditional context, she was free to choose the sung or spoken version, no matter what time of day it was.

Udegei girl in traditional dress.

Another tale from the shore dwellers tells about the relations between animals, explaining their behaviour. These animal tales have the same mythic origin, but a lighter tone.

CROW AND OTTER

There lived a crow. Every day she went hunting by the sea, turning over rocks, finding things to eat. When she found them she gobbled them up. She spent whole days going back and forth on the shore looking for food.

One time an otter came out of the water. "What are you

doing?" he asked.

"Oh, I'm just looking for food, catching little fish."

"Come visit me," said the otter.

"All right," said crow and she followed the otter under the ground. The otter got a pot, filled it with water and put it on the fire. And then he dove right into the water in the pot and disappeared!

The crow was waiting.

The otter came back bringing lots of fish. They ate and then the crow said, "*Anda*, my friend, next time you come and visit me."

A long time later the otter came to visit. So the crow thought, "How can I feed the otter? I'll just do what the otter did." So she thought a long time, walking back and forth. "Can I really dive into that hot water? Otter dove in just as it was coming to a boil. Ugh!"

But at last she made up her mind and dove in. Otter waited and waited, thinking, "When is that crow going to come back?" Then he saw the crow getting cooked.

"What a shame, I've lost my friend!"

The otter decided that from that time on he would feed the crows. And so from that time on, otter leaves half of what he catches on the shore for the crows to eat.

That's all! ▼

Valentina's two teenage daughters played musical instruments for us while the potatoes were cooking – long reed pipes, an elk call, a jaw harp, and a shaman's drum. These forest sounds felt out of place in the house, so we went outside. One of Valentina's daughters put on a shaman's belt, called *yampa*, made of leather in the form of a snake – one end is the snake's head and the other the tail. The belt was hung with cone-shaped bells that rang as the shaman or dancer swivelled her hips. She coordinated this movement with beating the drum and moving it up and down so that the bells on the inside of the drum also rang.

After supper the village children danced and sang at the

community hall against a backdrop of winning flower arrangements from a recent competition. The children's dance demonstrated a bear-hunt. Bears have long been held sacred by the peoples of the Amur region. The neighbouring Nivkh and Ul'chi peoples used to conduct a type of bear ceremony, where a bear cub was kept in the family and then ceremonially killed as a sacrificial messenger to the upper world.9 The Udegei did not have this ceremony, but they had one called "revenge on the bear," if a bear had harmed a human. The first Udegei writer, Jansi Kimonko, wrote about this ceremony, which took place in his childhood. A bear had killed a man, he says, and the people then pursued and killed the bear. In the ceremony a shaman translated the negotiations that took place between the bears and the hunter's brother. He learned that the bear had attacked the man because he had not obeyed the laws of the taiga: he had cursed the names of both bears and shamans. The people made an agreement that they would not break the laws in the future and the bears would not touch the hunters (Kimonko 1985, 63–5). The bones of the bear who had killed the hunter were scattered instead of being kept respectfully in one place so that they could return to the master of the taiga and take on new flesh. This bear would not return – his skull was hung in a tree as a warning.

Jansi Kimonko was later killed by a bear while hunting. There is a skull in the tree outside Valentina's house and I wondered if that skull had come from the same bear. Later I learned that it had not.

Valentina sang a song about Biatu, the name for a bear used only in Udegei songs and stories, not in ordinary speech. The name includes the idea that the bear is an evil spirit with a round moon-like face (Simonov 1998, 356). Biatu was invited home by Belye and given the best of everything. This song contains the first of many stories I heard about human marriage with bears and tigers. I have translated it in prose, which is how Valentina translated it to me, sum-marizing many verses.

BIATU AND BELYE

A girl lived with her brother as man and wife. One day while he was away, she called to the bear.

"You are my friend while my brother is away," she said. But then her brother tricks the bear: he sends Belye away and dresses in her clothing. The bear comes.

The girl gets mad and leaves her brother.

Then he gets sick of living alone and goes looking for his sister. On the way he meets two baby bears who come sniffing him saying, "Uncle, uncle, smells of uncle." He follows them and finds his sister.

She says, "The bear will come and kill you." He says he won't go away. She hides him.

The bear comes in and says, "It smells of a person here. Come out!"

The brother comes out and they all eat together. The bear challenges the man to go bear-hunting together. The man teases the two little bears and kills his sister's bear husband.

"Come back home with me," he says to her, "I acciden-tally killed your husband."

She says, "You did it on purpose. I won't go with you. Take the children and go away." She stays where she is and turns into a bear herself.

He lives with the children. When fall comes the chil-dren go to find a den. He follows and settles them down. He leaves an embroidered robe with them.

But in spring he comes back and sees blood every-where. Seven brothers have come. He finds them and says, "Why have you killed my nephews?"

"We didn't know."

"How could you not know? There was a robe hanging there."

"Don't be angry," they say.

He calls them to fight one by one. But instead they give him their sister as a wife and he goes home. ▼

As I look back on the bear song, I wonder what went wrong. The embroidered robe should have protected the babies, even if they were not wearing it. The designs around the openings and hems of clothing were meant to act as a protection against evil spirits, containing the love of the person who embroidered them. The positive images would not let evil in through those openings. Valentina emphasizes the fact that the hunters should have realized from the presence of the robe that these bears were part human. Perhaps the men were foreigners and didn't understand the meaning of the clothing, as is the case in the arctic story where a woman marries a whale and gives birth to a whale baby, which is later killed by hunters from another place who did not understand the mark she had put on her baby (Van Deusen 1999b, 139).

I only learned that the girl was living incestuously with her brother when Valentina explained the song more fully on her visit to Vancouver in 1998.[10] Incest is a difficult subject for society to deal with. Like most people, today's Udegei consider it a great sin. According to their traditions, a person must not marry within his/her own patriarchal clan. In earlier times, however, marriage between an older sister and younger brother was the norm (Simonov 1998, 25). Udegei myth says that a brother and sister were the only ones to survive a great flood, becoming the ancestors of the whole human race. Several stories tell of a girl who brings up a boy-child who is either orphaned or abandoned and then marries him.[11] These stories also refer to the flood tradition.[12]

Many stories have to do with the difficulties of finding a suitable spouse from a different clan when distances were great, resources changeable, and people constantly on the move. Both male and female initiation stories often include the search for an acceptable spouse and are similar to tales of shamanic initiation, which show the difficulties involved in finding and coming to terms with one's spirit helpers. There must have been times when the search failed and sisters lived with their brothers, their children becoming the future of the clan. Even as the structure of society and the interpretation of this relationship changed, the ancient form was retained in story.

The children of incest are often connected with bears. There are many tales in the Amur region of women marrying bears.[13] Sometimes the offspring are human, with almost superhuman powers, sometimes they are bears, and sometimes the mother gives birth to one of each. The children of bears (and tigers) are always twins, and twins are believed to have a sacred nature that can be traced back to the time of creation.[14] Valentina says that the important thing in this story is not the wrongness of incest but the fact that the hunters should not have killed the children.

Valentina showed us several beautiful embroidered dresses like the one mentioned in the story and pointed out various animals and the river in the designs. (Nanai designs tend to use more plant motifs than the Udegei.) She sees the borders as being like rivers, with the animals and birds living in them. It is easy to see the richness of the natural world reflected in the art work and there is an evocative similarity between the way the thread goes back over the same place more than once in the stitches and the repetition of words and images in story. A woman who has the ability to create these images is very powerful and a desirable marriage partner. The protective aspect of embroidered clothing – which probably comes from the creative energy that the woman puts into her work – and the power of the artist show up often in stories, like the story which follows about the ice mountain.

In this story the heroine, Belye, wears fishskin, which used

Detail of Udegei embroidery by Valentina Tunsyanovna
Kyalundzyuga, done over fishskin and showing a tiger face.

to be the most common material for summer clothing in the Amur. Women would dry the skins of salmon (and sometimes other fish) and carefully pound them until they became as supple as soft leather. They bleached some skins, which were naturally whitish after treatment, and dyed others using blue flowers. The blue pieces were cut into designs that the women appliqued onto white background skins – designs similar to those embroidered today. Salmon skin can be amazingly tough and is even used for the soles of shoes. Old Nanai log houses used fishskin as window panes.

Before the nineteenth century, when trade with China brought fabrics to the Amur region on a large scale, most summer clothing was made entirely of fishskin, while winter clothing was made of animal hides. The process of preparing fishskin is extremely labour intensive, and a woman might work several years on a robe that would last the rest of her life. Often she would be buried in the same robe she was married in, which she might have repaired many times, adding new decorations. Like the Nanai shaman Olga Beldi whom we met later on our journey (page 97), women would sometimes embroider several robes especially to be buried in, believing that they would use them to pay off various spirits they would meet on the way to the land of the dead. In the twentieth century some people started to pass these robes down in families, and many have been acquired by museums.

With the appearance of fabrics in the nineteenth century, which intensified in the twentieth, new clothing styles began to proliferate. Fabric appliques and embroidered designs were pieced onto fishskin robes, using the same deisn motifs that had previously been made of fishskin applique. Fabrics were cut into small pieces to make decorative patchworks or the fish scale patterns that had previously been made on winter clothing with mosaics of different colours of fur. Eventually women began to make clothing entirely of fabric, retaining the design motifs around borders and, in the case of a wedding dress, on the back, Udegei artists developed a technique of using silk threads to embroider over a design cut from fishskin. The fishskin, which is often folded and cut in the same way children make paper snowflakes, is not visible in the final result but makes the design stand out dramatically from the background. Nanai artists have developed the fabric applique more fully, often set off by embroidery. Ul'chi and Nivkh designs are identifiable by their unique motifs and the fact that their designs are more widely spaced on the background than those of their Nanai and Udegei neighbours.

Many of the design motifs represent animals and plants, while others are more abstract. Spirals appear frequently, as they do in ancient art all over the world. While it is possible to distinguish the motifs of the various peoples, each artist refines them in her own way. Local people always point out the beauty and fascination in their master artists' originality and endless invention.

Another layer of meaning in the image of clothing in the story of the Ice Mountain has to do with the fact that the Udegei used to tear the clothing of the dead in order to show the spirits in the next world that this person had come to stay.[15] Belye, in tearing off a piece of her clothing, is undergoing an initiatory death and rebirth, after which she gains the help of the Master of the Wind. Valentina told a second version of this story in 1997 in which she emphasized the practicality of Belye's clothing.

THE ICE MOUNTAIN[16]

A girl lived alone. She went hunting and fishing and she was also a great artist, sewing and embroidering all kinds of designs. One time she heard news that there was a mountain and on that mountain lived Yegdyga Doye, the Master of the Wind. The mountain was made all of ice and nobody could climb it. Anyone who tried would just fall back, it was so slippery. And on the top lived Yegdyga with his mother. If any girl could climb the mountain Yegdyga would marry her.

And so our Belye decided to go there. She put on her best fishskin robe with beautiful embroidered designs and over it she put a simple fishskin robe with no designs. She took a stick with a sharp animal claw lashed to the end, which could hook onto the mountain and hold her. And she went looking for the mountain.

She walked and walked and towards evening she came to a place where another girl lived. This girl said, "What news?"

Belye said, "I'm going to try the ice mountain, maybe I'll marry Yegdyga Doye."

The girl said, "I'll come too and try my luck."

Next day they got up early, cooked some food, and had breakfast. The other girl put on her best dress of satin but without designs, hoping that Yegdyga would choose her. The two of them walked and walked and towards evening they came to a third girl.

"What news?" she asked.

They said, "We've heard there's an ice mountain and that Yegdyga lives there and will marry whichever girl can climb to the top." And so the third girl decided to come too. The next day she dressed in her best Chinese silk and they set out.

Before long they came to the ice mountain. The sun was shining so brightly that its reflection on the ice hurt the eyes.

They started to climb. Yegdyga's mother was up on top and she noticed that three girls were coming, two of them all dressed up and the third in simple fish-skin.

She began to sing a song. "My son Doye, let the wind go, let it knock that girl in the fish-skin off our mountain so she won't get up here."

He let the wind go and it knocked the girl in the fancy dress off the mountain. But our Belye kept climbing with her stick, afraid of nothing. And the other girl was there too.

Again the mother began to sing. "Doye, Doye, see those girls! Let the wind knock the one in the fishskin off the mountain and the one in the beautiful dress climb up."

He let the wind go and it knocked that last girl off the mountain. Only Belye was left in the terrible wind. She bent further over and kept on climbing.

The mother was cursing, "Why did you knock the wrong ones off? Look, that girl in the old fishskin is still climbing!"

He made the wind stronger and stronger. He sent blizzard, snow, and darkness, but Belye bent further over and climbed and climbed. At last she got to the top. And then she took her stick with the hook and grabbed the door of their house, which was made of skin. She tore it off and threw it into the sea.

She went inside and sat down on Yegdyga's bed. He threw a knife at her to kill her. The knife wounded her leg.

She took a piece of embroidered cloth from her leggings where she had been wounded, left the design on the bed and went away.

She walked.

The mother noticed the design and called her son. "Look at this! What a fine artist she is, such a beautiful design. Go after her, son, catch her and marry her!"

Belye was going so fast that he couldn't catch up with her. And so he threw his spear and said, "Fly spear, and land in front of her so that she can't go any further."

The spear flew and fell before her. She wanted to step across it but he called out, "Don't cross that spear! It's a sin for a woman to step across a spear. That spear saves me in difficult moments."

She stopped out of respect for the spear, he caught up with her and healed her wound using his own saliva. And the wound healed, the blood stopped flowing. They went back and got married.

And that's how Belye defeated the Master of the Wind! ▼

Valentina told one last story that relates to life by the sea -
the tale of the hunter Yegdyga who married a seal.[17] The
story is full of themes of death and resurrection and story
has the form of a healing journey, with Yegdyga finding
helpers in three old women. Sagdi Mama is the deity who
brings the souls of children into bodies. While many may
think that the "red water of life" in the story represents
blood, Valentina takes a practical view, explaining that
there is a place in the taiga where the water is red, possibly
from mineral deposits.

YEGDYGA AND THE SEAL

Yegdyga lived with his wife on the shore of the sea. He
went fishing and one day he saw some seals. Yegdyga made
friends with a female seal who had come up on the rocks
to sun herself.

His wife was at home. He came back and after that he
was always finding fault with her - she was always doing
something wrong in his eyes.

She didn't understand. Things had been fine before. So
she followed him to find out what was happening. And she
saw how he came to the shore and called the seal. She saw
how the female seal came up and became like a second
wife to him.

When he came home and went to sleep, she cut him in
half right down the middle and attached one half onto
herself. She took his spear and went out onto the shore.

She called.

The seal thought, "That doesn't sound like his voice.
But who else can it be?" So she came up. The wife speared
her. The seal swam away, wounded.

The wife came home and put the halves of her husband
back together. Next day he went out and called, but the
seal didn't come. He got upset and dove into the water.

32

He found himself in another world. There was a path through the forest. He followed it and toward evening he came to an old woman.

"Grandmother," he said, "Have you seen my seal friend?"

The woman was old and grey. She said, "Yes, she came this way. I tended her wound and she went on. She was very ill."

He spent the night there and in the morning he went on. He came to an even older grandmother. She said, "Yegdyga, go on. You'll come to an even older woman and she is the one who knows."

He went on, following drops of blood. Sagdi Mama, the oldest woman of all, said, "She is dying. If you get there in time you can save her. I will tell you how. Not far from here you'll find red water. Take a bark container full of that red water and if you find her in time you can save her with the water."

He took red water from the river. He ran, shouting as he went so all could hear him. When he got there she was already on the way to the grave. Those carrying her were frightened by his shouting and they dropped her.

He poured the red water into the wound and she came to life. She woke up and said, "Oh, it's you. Who was it who tried to kill me?"

"My wife," he replied.

They started back. They got to the oldest of the three old women. Yegdyga went hunting and brought back meat. He dried it and left it for her. They went on to the second woman. They helped her with firewood and food. And also the third. And at last they got back to the land.

He didn't go back to his human wife. They moved to a different river to live. But people say that he was not able to live on land any more. He had to live in the water like a seal. Water creatures take people to themselves. ▾

2

More Stories from Gvasyugi

The next day was bright and sunny and we went fishing. I'm not much of a fisherman, but I love to ride in boats and walk in the woods so I took my camera and went along. Our guide was Alyosha, a rather shy, small man in his mid-twenties. The boat was an *ana*, a traditional Udegei dugout. Alyosha brought it in to shore using a pole, but once we got going he used a motor. Gvasyugi is located at the confluence of two small rivers, the Bulinka and the Gvasyuginka, which soon flow into the Khor. The Khor winds its way through the taiga for many kilometres before reaching the Ussuri, which flows into the Amur, which leads to the sea of Okhotsk. Many small rivers and streams join the big rivers; there are many turns, many rapids, many places to go astray. But Alyosha was completely at home on the river. He knew exactly which part of the stream to be in at any moment, where the shallow places were and the rapids. We left the village houses and barns and went upriver past grassy banks, haystacks, steep rock cliffs, evergreen and deciduous forests. An eagle circled overhead.

We pulled in to visit some of Alyosha's friends, who lived in a ghost town that looked a lot like the deserted mining towns of British Columbia. There were a number of old buildings, all falling in. Nadia recalled that when she was a child there was a real village here, with a store.

Three men were living in the house that was in the best shape. They had a battery-powered television set and I wondered if they watched the soap operas like everyone else. One man was a beekeeper, one a city dweller on summer vacation and the third I dubbed Dersu Usala after the famous Nanai guide who helped the prerevolutionary Russian geographer and ethnographer Arseniev as he surveyed the area in the early part of the twentieth century. Dersu Usala was an expert on life in the taiga – he showed Arseniev how to track and hunt, which plants to eat. And he saved the Russian's life by sheltering them in a haystack from a sudden storm. The Japanese film-maker Kurosawa brought the two to life in a wonderful film, named after Dersu, who is rumoured to have planted a secret ginseng plantation with many rare varieties somewhere in the taiga. Fortune-hunters are looking for it to this very day. Although Arseniev's stories have been read for generations in Russia as adventurous tales of life in the wilderness,[1] indigenous people today say that he betrayed their ancestors by disclosing their locations to the Tsarist government, who then came and killed them.

"Dersu Usala" lived all year round in a tent in the taiga, hunting and fishing. That day he was sitting outside, having a haircut. I had heard that there were people who had evaded Soviet society by living in the woods but had not expected to meet one.[2] But these men were not as isolated as I thought at first. During the hour we were there, two other fishing parties stopped in to compare notes on which fish were to be found where. They were also keeping an eye out for the man who was lost.

The three men shared lunch with us (with Nadia cooking!) and then we went further upstream, stopping here and there to try our luck with our fishing poles. At last we found a good spot and settled in. After awhile even I donned the hip boots and caught a couple of fish.

Then we started to cook and realized we had forgotten the salt. Alyosha said he'd go back to the beekeeper's and get some and I went along for the ride. Instead of going back the way we came, he took the boat a short way further upstream and then stopped – the river wound around and we could walk quickly across through the woods, saving gas. Alyosha pulled the boat in to shore, stuck his pole into the bank, and tied the boat to it. Once again I was struck by this simplicity and efficiency.

I like to think that I have a good sense of direction and can pick out landmarks and find my way in the woods. But I would never have found the beekeeper's place. There was no path and, although the trees were not large, the woods were deceptively dense. Sometimes we were pushing through bushes higher than our heads. Alyosha walked barefoot, with complete certainty, stopping here and there to show me berries to eat, pointing out those which were no longer good and those which were getting ripe. He showed me out where a bear had walked and dug. The day was warm and we heard birds and insects and smelled the fragrant grasses. He stopped and placed his hand on the ground. "This is where the bear was sleeping in the sun," he said. "See where she laid her head."

We got the salt and came back. By this time a good fire was going on the pebbly spit and the potatoes and fish were almost done. On the way home we stopped and picked cedar cones and ate the nuts for desert.

The thing that impresses me most about the traditional Udegei way of life is that everything they made was small and efficient. They are a small people and they walk lightly. Their traditional houses were small and could be built

Irina Ivanovna Kimonko, embroidery artist. Village of Gvasyugi.

quickly and left behind. They kept their food in small birchbark containers, whose smell preserved the food and whose carved designs enhanced the home. Their barns, even today, are placed on stilts to keep mice out. Even while living in Soviet-style houses the Udegei seem to prefer sitting on small stools at small tables, spending every possible moment outdoors.

Irina Ivanovna Kimonko, one of the finest embroidery artists, told us of a journey she made with her family at the age of eight. They were going over the mountains to visit relatives who lived beside the sea. Her younger sister was in a cradle on her mother's back. Her father had a second wife and they all went together. They went upstream by boat and then on foot. When they came to a place where people

37

prayed, every woman tied a piece of cloth to a tree.[3] They made a little house and the children were not allowed inside. But Irina looked. She saw three poles and a figure with eyes, nose, and mouth. The adults placed food on a little table and burned the ledum plant (Labrador tea), which is used by shamans in their rituals. They prayed for a good trip to a new place, to a new family.

They went down a very steep hill and came to the village of Samarga on foot. They visited for several months. When it was time to come back, the older wife didn't want to go back, so they left her behind. The whole trip took about half a year, and they arrived back in March. On the way home they made sleds for themselves up on the mountain pass, put all the food and children on them, and came back down.

Tosia said that when she was a girl in the thirties there were no villages and people lived scattered in the taiga. The government created the villages and said that people had to move there, so they took apart the houses they were in at the time and floated them down the river on rafts.

Her stories reminded me of those Jansi Kimonko – who came from Gvasyugi – had written, telling about how his grandfather came over the mountains following the tracks of an otter and found the river Sukpai and later the Khor. He also told of floods and forest fires and about their adaptation to a new life in the early Soviet period. Kimonko's sister, Evdokia Batovna Kyalundzyuga or Auntie Dusia, was still living in Gvasyugi. One of the most respected elders of the village, she told stories and made her own thread for sewing hide clothing out of moose sinew. She still stuck a knife into the threshold at night to protect her home.

Dusia told a long story that I found hard to understand at first, owing to her lack of teeth and my difficulty with her unfamiliar use of the Russian language. One thing that was confusing was that, like many speakers of Tungus languages, Dusia confuses the Russian pronouns for "he" and "she." Her own language does not make this distinction in speaking of people. I listened to the story first in Udegei and then in Russian. Even in the original, which I understood not at all, I had the sense of moving along a river, a movement that is absolutely central to the life of river nomads.

Luckily she repeated the story when I visited her again two years later and this time I was able to put the missing pieces in place. Her story explains how a very ancient kind of house was made of bones, customs surrounding bear ancestry and the eating of bear meat, and the incest taboo.[4] Here both brother and sister must think about how to find a spouse, since they have no neighbours. Auntie Dusia imbues her telling with an air of mystery and slyness and she gets a lot of pleasure from talking about the girl's three husbands!

SISTER AND BROTHER

A brother and sister lived together. They grew up and started to live.

One day the sister said, "Let's look for people to live with. A wife for you and a man for me. How can we go on living like this?"

There was no one living near them.

He said, "Where will I find someone? Maybe up-stream, maybe down."

It seems to me this must have been in winter. The brother thinks, "Where will I find someone? My sister says I have to. I don't know anybody. There's no one nearby. All right. This morning early, I'll go." He says to his sister, "Make my breakfast early."

"Why?"

"I'm going. If you won't do it for me, I'll have to go look for a wife."

She had been dreaming for a long time of marrying her brother. She got up early and boiled food.

They went outside.

"Where will I go?" said the brother. "There's no one nearby. Where to go, up-stream or down? All right I'll go down."

As soon as he was gone she went back inside and got ready to go herself. And she too went down-stream. After her brother? Nobody knows. She won't go by the river but will fly or something up in the air. She got ahead of him. She probably flew. They travelled and travelled. She went up and he went down.

Then it was time to stop for the night. They stopped. He says, "We had everything at home; firewood, everything. I should go back there." Not above but below. He thinks, "Where will I spend the night, there's nothing here."

Then below he saw smoke and a hut. People must be there. He went and looked. It was exactly like their place; a barn, firewood, a house. "Whoever lives here is just like us!" he thought.

He approached. No dogs. A woman came out. (His sister got there first.) He thinks, "She looks exactly like my sister!"

She says, "Where did you come from? Nobody ever comes here, not even a crow, not even a bird. Nobody at all."

"My sister said I should go looking for a wife. That's why I left home."

She got cooking! They ate. And all the time it was his sister! She disguised herself, or fooled him.

"I don't care where I go, I just need to find a wife," he said.

"But I want to get married too! There are no people near here," she said. They ate, and then sat and talked, but he was embarrassed because she was exactly like his sister.

"It's hard for me living here alone," she says. So in a moment he agreed to stay with her, and they lay down to sleep.

After some time had passed he said, "I need to go see my sister," and he went up to see how she was doing. Maybe she has no firewood, he thought. But somehow he

Evdokia Batovna (Dusia) Kimonko. Udegei storyteller,
village of Gvasyugi.

didn't want to go. He probably felt in his soul that something was wrong.

And she said, "Why don't you go see your sister. Go tomorrow. Maybe she's hungry, maybe she died."

So he went.

As soon as he was gone she got things together and flew back there where they had lived before. She took everything, the barns, the firewood, the house.

He got there and stopped, thinking, "My sister is probably not alive." But then he saw smoke. "Thank god she's alive."

He came to the house, and she came out, "Oh brother, here you are alive. I thought you were dead."

She cooked dinner. They ate.

"How are you?" she asked, and in fact she had married her brother!

"Oh, I don't know. I met somebody exactly like you. Her dress, the house, all exactly like ours."

"Oh, there are all kinds of people," she said.

He didn't feel like going back to his wife. Instead he went hunting, thinking, "What is this all about?"

"Why don't go back to your wife?" asked his sister.

"There's something wrong. She's just like you in every way, even her dress."

"Oh, there are all kinds of people."

Again she says, "Why don't you go back? After all, you're married."

"Yes, there's something wrong. She's just like you."

She wanted to be married to him again.

"All right," he said, "I'll go tomorrow."

As soon as he was gone, she flew away in an instant. She took everything, barns, house, firewood.

He thought, "Who knows if my wife is alive?" Then he saw the smoke. "Thank god she's alive."

"Was your sister alive?" asked his wife.

"Yes, she's fine."

Still that feeling that something's wrong.

So they started to eat.

"How's your sister?"

"Fine."

Time went by and she gave birth to a boy and a girl. I don't remember which was first. And he went hunting every day, killing all the animals until there was nothing left nearby. He had killed everything. So he had to go further, to the place where he had lived before. And there he killed a moose.

Why he was like that and got fooled, I don't know.

He killed the moose and started dragging it home whole. When he got close to home he left it there. On purpose. He didn't take the skin off. He didn't know, but he probably felt something. He left his arrow there in the moose.

He said, "If I am really living with my sister, I'll have killed her. I'll leave my arrow here. If I am really living with my sister, there will be a mark on her chest."[5]

"Where have you been for so long? We are hungry waiting for you," his wife said when he returned.

"I was far away and killed a moose. I brought him home whole. Tomorrow, son, you take the sled and go get it."

The son agreed. The next day the boy went out and a bird talked to him.

He came back and said, "Mama make me an arrow. I want to kill a bird."

She says, "Don't go far."

He went and shot a bird. The bird started to speak in the Udegei language. "What a bad family!" said the bird. "A brother is living with his sister and now the boy is doing this to me."

The boy ran home.

"Mama, I went along the river and I shot a bird who talked." He told her what the bird said.

"When your father comes home, don't tell him."

He didn't say anything. His father came home late. They started to eat.

"Papa, today I went down the river …"

"Don't bother your father."

She must have guessed. So they finished eating. She was very tired and lay down. She lay down early.

And then papa said to his son, "What did you want to say before, while we were eating?"

"Oh papa, I went along the river and shot a bird and almost killed it. But I just hit the fluff. She talked and said, "That woman is living with her brother."

Next morning the mother cooked and then took the sled and went off into the taiga.

The father said, "You'll go a long way, I didn't go that far. There's no animal to take you there."

"Never mind, there will be tracks."

They waited and waited and she didn't come back. He guessed she was that animal that he had shot.

They ate, but then he couldn't sleep and went outdoors. But she had taken the sled.

He walked and walked. And then he saw her lying there dead. He took out his arrow and took the moose. He left his wife.

He got home and it was dark, the children were crying – there was no fire and no light. He didn't go inside but made a fire outside. He lived there for several days and didn't feed his children and didn't eat himself. To live with your own sister is a sin.

He was a long time there outside, without going into the hut. Finally he loaded up the sleigh, made a cut through the ankle of each child, put a strap through and hitched them to the sleigh. He tied them to the sled. The girl too, she was also there.

And off he went.

He drove those children day and night, without a break, without food. He went and went and at last the boy tore off at that place where he was attached and fell down. He died. But the girl stayed there with her father. She pulled and pulled and pulled and also got torn off at the ankle.

44

He didn't realize it and left her behind.
She cried there. "Where's papa?"
Then a brown bear came along.
"Why are you crying?"
She told him what her papa had done.
"Don't cry, I'll take you home."
She got up on his back.
"Hold on tight."
It was dark.

"There is my house," said the bear. It was that thing that bears make. He took her to his den but stopped outside. "I won't take you in there. You'll sleep here. I'll dig in there and you stay here. Tomorrow I'll make you a house."

He got up in the morning and started bringing in wood. He made the house well. All good on the outside, with a nice bed inside. "Don't be afraid of me," he said. "I won't do anything bad to you."

They lived there, and she grew up.

Then he said, "Now I'm going to find you a husband. I'll find you the very best. Just don't worry and don't go away. Every day I'll go looking."

He looked and looked. Once he saw the tracks of Merge, a hunter – the man's tracks went one way and the bear's crossed them. He went home to his den. He went through the hole in the wall of her house, to his own place.

He explained this. "First people will come, hunters. You tell them you are alone, that there's no one here. If they ask about my den, say it just is like that."

And he went away.

Toward evening one young hunter came. Looking at the hole in the wall, that hunter said, "What is this?"

"Ahh, it's just like that. When I first started to live here it was already like that."

She fooled him.

They got ready to spend the night. She cooked, they ate. He asked again, what is that outside, and she didn't tell him.

"It was like that when I was small," she said.

"How do you live, alone?"

"As I remember, when I was little I started to live alone. My father and mother died." She fooled him.

They ate.

He asked, "Are you alone?"

"Alone."

"I'm alone too," he said, "I have no one, I'm alone in the woods. Let's get married."

She had already grown up.

"All right, let's."

"You're alone and I'm alone. I have no parents." And so he stayed.

Next day he went hunting. The bear came home and said to her, "Today I will test him to see if he is strong. Don't you be afraid. Don't tell him that I am a bear. I'll cry out and he will jump out to see what is happening and freeze."

The bear went out. "If he kills me, don't you eat my meat. These two places only you can eat and nothing else." He showed her the places on his buttocks and then went away.

Again the man came. They lay down to sleep and talked.

Then from outside, that brown bear cried out. The fellow didn't put anything on but ran out in his bare feet. He didn't come back. She was afraid and waited til morning to go out. The man was scared and froze to death. In the morning she went out – "Oh the poor thing," she said, looking at him.

Then the bear came again in the evening.

"Why did you do that, to kill a person?" she asked.

"I told you I will find you a very very strong man. Brave, not afraid of anything. Again I will come and bring a hunter. Don't tell him anything and don't be afraid. I want to find you a very kind person so you will live well."

The bear went away.

Again in the evening a fellow came. You could see from his tracks that he was stronger than the first. He came in to sleep. He was stronger than the other one.

"Let's spend the night," he said.

They ate and he asked, "Are you alone?"

"I'm alone."

"What's that hole there?"

"Oh, I remember when I was little it was already there." She was fooling him. Again she agreed to get married and they lay down. They talked.

Again the bear cried out, the fellow ran out barefoot to kill the bear, but he didn't succeed. It was dark, scary, how could she go out? She also didn't hear the bear's voice. She sat and sat there that night and when it got light she went out. The man had frozen there beside the threshold. He wanted to shoot but didn't succeed.

Again she asked the bear and he said, "I told you long ago that I would find you someone strong." He went into the taiga.

Toward evening he came, that brown one.

"Girl, again I found tracks and these must be even stronger." He came and said, "I found this man ..." That's what he said.

And then he went away, without eating. Again a man came - he was good-looking! Strong, young.

"Are you alone?" he asked.

"Yes, I've always been alone. I remember when I was little I was already alone."

"How do you get your food and firewood?"

"They come to me themselves."

This man asked, "Who do you live with?"

"With no one."

"What is that hole?"

"When I was little I remember it was like that. I don't know."

"When you were little who brought you up?"

"I don't know."

"Well, if you don't have anyone, lets get married."

Again they lay down to sleep, this was the third time already! They started to tell about how they had lived. Then suddenly that bear cried out. This Merge didn't run right out but quickly got dressed and then went out.

He came back and said, "Girl, I don't know if you want to kill me. I don't know if it was your father or brother, but I killed him."

She said, "He said someone would come and kill him."

"Who was he to you?"

She didn't tell.

A man had lived with his sister and given birth to a boy and a girl.

In the morning she went out. Right there on the threshold he had killed the bear. He was such a strong man.

"As you like, if you want to kill me," he said.

"I am a woman, how can I kill you? He ordered it himself. He told me to use the bones to make a house, to take the skin and everything. The skin will cover the house. He told me to take the meat from those two places but nowhere else. You, of course, can eat the rest."

"Who was he, your father?"

She didn't tell.

They started to live well. It turned into the kind of house our people used to live in. They lived and she gave birth to a boy and a girl as her mother had. They both lived, the two of them.

And the small one said, "I will tell you part of the way we lived – the most awful thing. Papa killed mama. Why, I don't know. Her brother killed her. He was a bear, not people. I don't know. They lived together a long time and she gave birth to a boy and a girl."

Once a man came to their place, thin, torn, all ragged and in bad shape. He was her father. How would she know this was her father? She wanted to bring him home. It's cold to live outside, to sleep, prepare firewood.

But he didn't stay. "I'll turn into a deer," he said, and went to live in the taiga. ▼

Arseniev recorded several versions of this tale almost a hundred years ago. In them the bear marries the girl, and her brother survives and marries a tiger. Later he accidentally kills the bear while hunting. (In Arseniev's time women were forbidden to eat the meat of bears killed by their brothers.)

People say that the girl who lived with the bear was the original ancestor of the Udegei people. In Arseniev's story it is clear that the children of incest are sacred ancestors of whole peoples, while in the story of Biatu and Belye the children's function is more problematical. Perhaps if they had survived they too might have become ancestors of new clans, as is often the case in stories where women marry animals. These stories are similar to stories of women in the Arctic who refuse to marry. Some of them marry whales, which leads to the tragic death of their children, while others go on to found new clans (Van Deusen 1999b, 39).

Dusia told two more stories that day. The first is about a girl who married a crow. This is a pattern repeated many times in Amur stories with different animals and even objects.[6] It has something in common with stories of Beauty and the Beast. In Amur stories, as in some European ones, the girl's anger is the catalyst that turns the animal (or crow) to a man. The story also emphasizes that before he could marry a foreign man had to prove to a girl's family that he could provide a living.

THE GIRL WHO MARRIED A CROW

Some sisters lived alone, apart from their parents. They lived properly – they hung their blankets out every day to air. One day the youngest sister went outside and saw that her blanket had fallen. Why? A crow fell out of her blanket. She didn't tell anyone. She didn't hang it up any more, she just folded it up.

One day she went out for firewood and while she was gone her sisters looked in the blanket, saw the crow, and told their parents. The father said, "Can she really be like that, living with a crow? I'll kill the crow. And drive her out!"

The girl left home. She cried. She took the blanket with the crow rolled up inside and went away. "How will I live?" she thought. "Where can I go? If I go back my father will kill me." She found a good place and made a tent. The crow never showed himself. She would leave him a bowl of food but didn't see him.

In the spring she got sick of it. "I don't know what I'm living for," she thought. "I have nobody to talk with or laugh with." So she didn't cook anything. She got mad and slept for a long time. When she woke up it was already light in the house. She went outside and it was dark, the moon was shining. "How can this be?" she thought. "Am I dreaming?" She went back in and saw a man sleeping there, shining with the light of his beauty. She came up to him and he jumped.

"I won't live alone," she said.

He said "All right," and turned into a man.

He went hunting.

He told her, "Go and tell your parents to come here. Tell them the crow has killed a wild boar. Invite them to come and eat."

She put on her best dress and went to see her parents (but not her sisters!).

"Where did you come from?" they asked. "Are you alive?"[7]

She was silent. Finally she said, "The crow is calling you."

She went away. After that they laughed. How could a crow kill a boar? The next day they went to see their daughter. "Let's just go and look," they thought. They saw the crow and went away.

Again the girl awoke at night and it was light and warm in the house. She went outside and it was dark. She looked and saw that it was not her house. She looked up and everything was so beautiful, there were gold and silver cuckoos sitting there. Everything was clean. A silver and gold fence surrounded the house.

"Let's get up and talk," she said.

"I'm shy," he replied. He took off his crow feathers and she hid them.

"What? Am I going to live alone all my life?"

"All right," he agreed, "we will live together."

The next day the sisters and the mother and father came and saw the beautiful house. The father and mother came in but not the sisters.

"Papa and mama, where are my sisters?" she asked.

"They didn't come."

She looked out and saw that they had hung themselves from shame.

There was a party to celebrate the wedding. Seven days and nights they ate and drank. Then the crow man said, "I will pay for your daughter." He gave the parents lots of money. The father says, "I'm old," and the man gave them enough to last the rest of their lives. They went away.

I can't remember if those young people had any children or not. ▾

The next story reflects the myth that humans originated in trees. One Nivkh creation myth attributes the differences among tribes to their origin in the sap of various trees. In this case the child born of a tree turns out to be an evil spirit, a theme that also comes up in Nivkh myth.

The image of bones containing both positive and negative life force is particularly powerful in this story. The girls' dog saves their lives by giving up his own so that his bones can create a bridge. Later, after being washed away by the river, the bones reappear in one place, ready to be of service again. It seems possible that the dog might come back

to life after helping the girls back across the river. The
bones of the evil creature, however, must be burned in
order to get rid of him once and for all.

TWO SISTERS

There were two sisters. The older one was very smart,
calm, and an artist. She sewed all kinds of fine designs and
dresses. The other one did nothing.

They lived. One day the older one said, "Let's look for
a son."

"Where?"

"In the taiga."

So they each made a cut on a tree but they didn't find
anything. They kept looking, each one alone. At last one
of them cut a tree and it was red. They cut it down. There
was a little boy crying there. They took him home to their
kava, washed him, and made him a cradle. They took
good care of him. He grew and started to smile and laugh.

They went out for firewood. The boy was laughing and
picking things up. Then the house started to move. It
almost fell down. The house itself started talking. Something fell – it was not level.

One sister said, "Why did we make it like this?"

"We made it this way so the snow would fall off. But now
probably there is something in our house. I'll go out, you
hide."

She went out for fire-wood. Nobody was there. Then the
house itself spoke. "I should have eaten them long ago," it
said. "I'm suffering. They hold me and tie me."

The house almost fell.

The older sister told the younger about it. "Our son is
an *amba*. He says he should have eaten us long ago, he
should have killed us. What shall we do?" There were just
the two of them, they had no neighbours.

52

"Let's go home and light the fire. We'll boil water. We'll tell him we are going to wash him. When it boils I'll put the child in."

So they prepared. "You hold him," said one sister.

Then they heard his voice saying, "I should have killed them long ago." The sister was ready. They put the baby in the pot.

They went away. They rode day and night on a dog sled. They came to the river. How could they get across? Then their dog said, "Kill me and put my bones across the river. The bones will make a bridge." The dog said to use his bones, to kill him. When the *amba* came the bones would be gone.

They crossed. They were sorry for the dog, but they had to get away. They crossed and by the time the *amba* came the bones had washed away.

Night came but they made no fire – they were scared. They made a little house. One night a mouse came. "Go look at my barn. Something is alive in there. Help me."

The elder sister took the scraper and went to look. She said to the mouse, "Ask it where it hurts."

It was night. There was nothing to see. They heard a voice saying, "Oh, I should have eaten them long ago. Help me, mouse. These women burned me."

"Where do you hurt?" asked the mouse.

"This place hurts, lower down."

She threw the scraper at that place. Then she came back out of the barn.

"Sister, he was alive. I don't know if I killed him."

They continued to live.

Finally one of them said, "Alive or not let's go back and look. Has he come over to this side? How could he have crossed?"

The dog had said, "If you have trouble, call my bones." The bones were gathered on the shore. Now one sister said, "Help me to get across, to go home. Make a bridge."

The bridge appeared. They went across.

Anna Dinchuevna Kimonko (centre) with her husband and daughter. Anna was one of the first heads of village administration under communism. She embroidered all the clothes they are wearing.

They looked and saw that there was no smoke coming from their house. Probably he died, they thought.

"I'll just go and look," said the elder sister. "Leave the sled far away."

She went in and he was dead.

"Sister," she called, "he is dead. What will we do with him?"

"Let's burn his bones."

They prepared wood outside and pulled him out. They threw him in the fire and burned him. After that they lived well.

No men around! ▼

Three days after he went missing from Gvasyugi, the drowned man's body was found. It was the beekeeper who found him. By chance I found out that the beekeeper's wife was the school librarian. It surprised me that he had a wife, after seeing him at the ghost town. Clearly I had a lot to learn about how people live here.

Parallel to this death was the drowning of a cow, who must have stumbled into the river and got her horns caught in overhanging branches. This, too, was a great loss for a family.

People cooked food in preparation for the funeral. Everyone in Tosia's kitchen seemed to have a headache except me and I had a stomachache that I attributed to some moose fat that I had eaten out of politeness the day before. We had visited Anna Dinchuevna, also a fine embroidery artist, who had a terrible headache that no one could cure. All sorts of doctors and extrasensory healers had tried, but the only person who had had any effect was the Nanai shaman Mingo Geiker in the village of Naikhin on the Amur. Nadia urged Anna Dinchuevna to send Mingo a bottle of vodka or a small article of her own to allow her to continue her healing, since we would be in Naikhin soon and could take it with us. But she refused and the headache raged on. Anna Dinchuevna was a devoted Communist Party member and did not consult shamans.

The sky was grey, a thunderstorm on the way. People were talking about death. Nadia said that if it is sunny for a funeral it means the deceased was a bad person and vice versa. There were interesting cross-currents here. The day might turn out sunny and there might also be a thunderstorm.

No one stayed on the subject of death for long. Instead they talked about shamans. Tosia told about shamans gathering in living rooms for competitions. She recalled a woman who swallowed hot coals and a man who could be shot through the chest with an arrow. If it were pulled out at the right time he would survive, if not he would die, like a yogi.

Shamans did not use plants for healing, she explained. Other people did, however, and the choice and preparation of plants remained family secrets. If the secret got out, the plant would lose its effectiveness. Some of these plant remedies are forgotten but many are still in use.

Dusia came into the kitchen. She talked about how smallpox bacteria can stay around for a hundred years. There were terrible epidemics in her grandfather's time, she said. Many many people died. If someone came down with smallpox, everyone else would move away. There was one woman who took her children and went off into the taiga and survived there all winter in a hut that she built herself. She set traps and caught animals for food. When the epidemic was over, Dusia's grandfather went out and brought them back.

The funeral was due to start in about an hour and Valentina told us about her own father's funeral. "The coffin was made out of planks and all the local artists came and painted designs on it to send off with their last wishes. A female shaman accompanied his soul to the other world, *Buni*. She described descending through a hole in the earth. People were holding her by a strong rope around her waist. They went through darkness until it got light. The seasons there were the opposite to what they are here. Then a man came out to meet and welcome Valentina's father. It was someone of the dead man's clan, maybe his own father. People present at the ceremony asked questions to determine exactly who it was. Then the shaman left him there and came back – the people were pulling on the rope. She rested and the conversation returned to normal." In earlier times people built a special burial hut and left the body in it and moved away. They did not go near that place again for fear of evil spirits.

Then Valentina broke into a smile and told us another thing that happened at that funeral. Before his death, her father had requested that he be buried in some special Chinese underwear that he had. One son had brought it back from the army. When the time came, Valentina thought, "Who'll know the difference?" It was brand new, good stuff, and she didn't put it on him. Sure enough, at the funeral her father spoke through the shaman and said, "Give me some cloth from the locked trunk and why didn't you bury me in that underwear?" Of course Valentina was the only person who understood what it was about, and she was embarrassed to admit to having saved the underwear.

For the drowned man's funeral, the sun was in and out. Perhaps, like most of us, he had been neither all good nor all bad.

3

Nivkh Storytelling in Nikolaevsk-na-Amure

Nadia and I returned to Khabarovsk and from there flew two hours to the city of Nikolaevsk-na-Amure, at the mouth of the Amur River. On the *Meteor*, or hydrofoil it would have taken about two days, and by steamer, a week. Alla Kondin-ko, whom I already knew from my original trip to Sakhalin, came to meet us at the airport. Alla was running a success-ful performing ensemble in this small city, whose history as a trading port goes back to Tsarist times. The indigenous people here are the Nivkh, a small minority in the city, who also live in northern Sakhalin. Although culturally related to their neighbours up the Amur, the Nivkh language is an isolate and they have been in the area much longer than their neighbours. They also have cultural links with the peoples of Kamchatka and with the Ainu of Japan.[1]

We soon met Maria Semynovna Pimgun. I am 5′5″ and she came to somewhere between my elbow and shoulder.

Gonyaina and Maria Semyonovna Pimgun. Nikolaevsk na Amure.

Then in her mid-sixties, in her youth she had suffered from a bone disease that left her legs turned outwards. Although she walked slowly with a cane she never mentioned any discomfort and stood straight. She seemed to be cheerfully tying to shock us with her cursing, smoking, and general outspokenness and stayed up half the night gambling with friends at a game similar to Bingo but with refinements that included joking word substitutions. Like her friends, Maria Semyonovna had a phenomenal memory for numbers.

   Inflation had reduced the ruble to near worthlessness – everything was being counted in hundreds.[2] While this made supporting a family nearly impossible, it was convenient for recreational gamblers, who used the old one and three ruble notes in their games. In the course of the evening I was relieved of my entire supply of rubles and also learned a lot about games. In the old days it was forbidden for women to do any work while the men were away hunting or fishing since it would bring bad luck. Instead the women would gather in one house and play games and tell stories. The noise they make is designed to distract the forest spirits so they won't notice that the men are hunting. This must explain the gusto with which they throw themselves into it!

I'd seen their enthusiasm before, at the festival on Sakhalin the previous year. Jerry Alfred, a northern Tuchone singer from the Yukon, had taught a simplified version of the stick gambling game as it is played in the Canadian North. It was supposed to be a brief demonstration but the Nivkh women immediately caught on and started adding hilarious variations of their own. They would certainly have played all night if the organizers had not called a halt.

Maria Semyonovna's family were seal hunters. She was born in 1932 in Kasyanovka and lived in the village of Kuklya which, like many other villages, no longer exists. The Soviet government had a great penchant for making plans on paper and then moving whole villages from one place to another with no particular regard to the suitability of the new locations or the difficulties involved for those who were moved. The policy has resulted in a series of ghost towns and a general sense of uprootedness in the population.

Maria Semyonovna recalled hearing stories from her uncle, who could tell some that lasted two nights. You can make up a tale, she said, but it would be a sin to make up a legend.[3] She also recalled a holiday at the spring breakup, when people went out along the ice to feed the spirits of the Amur.

The tale of Maria Semyonovna told about why the Nivkh had no writing before the Soviet period is a typical example of her sense of humour. Although the Nivkh resisted the attempts of Russian missionaries in the nineteenth century to convert them to Christianity, it appears they were not averse to adapting a good story![4]

Ceremony to feed the spirit of the land, Sakhalin Island.
(Photo by Murray Pleasance.)

NIVKH WRITING

Some people made a brick staircase. At this time everybody understood each other's languages. Other peoples, animals, birds, everybody. They were interested in getting writing, so they built this staircase to heaven. They were going to ask god for writing.

So up they went. But along the way they started not to understand each other – first the animals, then other people. God was punishing them for coming up. People of various nationalities were there, each with his own language now.

They had to decide which one would go on. It was a Nivkh who finally went. He knew the taiga, he knew everything, so he was selected to go to god. The man went through the mountains, the sea, the forest, over the rainbow, everywhere.

He got there.

God agreed to give people writing. All the peoples were waiting below. Of course the Nivkh wanted our language to be first, so he put our writing on top of the pile. Russian was at the bottom.

He crossed the sea on a dolphin, on a whale, and got almost all the way home. But then it started to rain, to pour! The pages got all wet. He stood under a tree but couldn't help getting the writing wet. He made a fire and dried the papers out. Some of the writing survived, the ones on the bottom, but the ones on top, all our peoples' writing, got wet. That's why we don't have writing and the Russians do. ▼

While the image of the staircase to heaven obviously comes from the Christian Bible, other elements are humorously adapted from Nivkh culture: for instance, understanding the language of the animals was a much-valued skill of hunters, who were often said to approach the upper world by going to high places in the mountains. The story inverts the Russian perspective, since they called the Nivkh "primitive" because of their illiteracy.

Maria Semyonovna took us to see her friend Klavdia Ivanovna Tidip, who was born in 1931. She was looking after her two young grandsons that day, who sat with us in her kitchen while she told this story.

KNEE BUMP (SWAN GIRL)

There lived an old man and an old woman. One evening the old woman went outside. She opened the door, then some kind of rock bumped against her knee. Oh, how it hurt! She grabbed her knee and went indoors.

"What happened to you?" asked her husband.

"Oh, how it hurts!" she said, and her knee started to puff up. So they made her a bandage, drank some tea and went to bed. But the old woman woke up in the night from pain. She looked at her knee and the bump was round like a egg.

Early in the morning she woke up and unwrapped the bandage. The egg fell off. They wrapped the egg, and the next morning out came a little boy! They were happy, and wrapped him up in Chinese silk and took care of him.

The boy grew fast, not by the day but by the hour. On the third day he said to the old man, "Make me a bow and arrow, I want to go hunting."

The old man said, "How will you hunt? You're still little. You need to grow."

But the boy went out and brought back game. First small birds, then a duck, and then one of the two small swans who flew by. Later the parents found the swan feathers outside. Then they ate and slept.

Next day they woke up and there on the bench lay a beautiful girl with long braids.

"A guest! Where did she come from?" said the mother.

"What a beauty! Her braids reach to the ground," said the father. They tried not to wake her.

The girl heard them and woke up. They asked her where she came from.

"An old man showed me the way and I came to you. He said if you were sleeping when I got here I should lie down and sleep too. And so I did."

Well, the young people liked each other. They got married and lived long and happily. ▼

Klavdia's story has a lot in common with many Turkic stories in which an orphan boy marries a swan girl after stealing her feathers. This connection with stories from thousands of kilometres away is not as strange as it seems at first glance, and may have come from two directions. First, the languages of several Amur peoples (although not the Nivkh) belong to the Tungus branch of the Altai family, to which the Turkic languages also belong. The Tungus peoples moved into the far east around 3,000 years ago from the area around Lake Baikal and the Sayan Mountains, bringing their stories with them. Today's southern Tungus peoples, who now inhabit the Amur region, were evicted from their earlier homeland at that time, replaced by warlike Turkic and Mongolian peoples who were moving into the Baikal-Sayan area from further to the south. Other Tungus language peoples, the Even and Evenk, still live widely scattered across most of Siberia. A second connection came more recently, when the Mongols, whose storytelling traditions have much in common with those of the Turkic peoples, invaded the area of the lower Amur in thirteenth century.

We travelled to the village of Mago, where Maria Semyonovna had friends. Mago is on an island in the Amur, some two hours' drive from the city. We crossed to the island on a motor-launch. I cringed when I saw the pier – boards had rotted out and there were big holes. We had to climb up from the last rotting board over the water to the deck of the boat. Could Maria Semyonovna make it? Would we lift the little old lady bodily?

The situation didn't faze her. She just handed her cane to the person who had gone before her, took a hand, and pulled herself up. I had to laugh, thinking of the hilarious tale I had heard of her absolute refusal to get on the metro in Leningrad when she went there to perform with a dance ensemble. She had to be coaxed through the turnstile and onto the escalator. In the end an unknown man picked her up and deposited her on the train. She cursed loudly in Nivkh and then made a show of being embarrassed, so that even those who didn't understand the language would know that she had cursed. Here on the boat things were different – she was simply enjoying an outing on home territory.

On the island a woman named Rima and her mother shared their home with us. Rima, in her late thirties, had worked for twenty years in the sawmill that had closed the year before, leaving the whole town unemployed. She exuded the strength, forthrightness, and energy of a person accustomed to physical work. Now she had a boring job sitting at the desk at the local dormitory, where a room was much cheaper and easier to get than an apartment.

She laughed with us as two elderly local women told about going to dances in heavy cork boots. During the second world war these women had had to leave their usual work fishing and growing potatoes to go logging. They spent several years felling trees by hand and cork boots were all they had.

Rima told us with both humour and rage about her mother's three marriages. The first time she was given, or perhaps sold, to a much older man who had come back from World War II in terrible condition. Why would parents marry their daughter to such a man unless for money, Rima asked? "My mother nursed the man and brought him back to life. Then he went away to work in another area. There he met a woman who put a spell on him. He stayed there with her. He knew that he needed to return to his wife, but he couldn't. Eventually he came back on a fishing trip and took the opportunity to hang himself where his young wife would be the one to find him. Took the easy way out," Rima concluded scornfully.

The second husband was Rima's father. He told her mother, "Until you give me a son, I won't marry you." Three daughters were born.

I didn't find out what happened to him in the end, but the third husband was a Korean, the father of Rima's brother. The brother was watching TV while his mother brought in millends, cut them, and stacked them for firewood. "Lazy," said Rima. "He's the reason I installed a good lock on the door!"

I didn't find out what became of the third husband either, nor did I hear anything about the father of Rima's daughter, who was home on vacation from medical school. Instead Rima told about how much she loves to go ice fishing in winter. She dresses warmly and walks an hour or so out to the river. She doesn't mind getting cold as she sits there with her illegal triple hook through a hole in the ice – she knows she'll get warm on the way back and have good fresh fish with winter potatoes for supper.

While we were in Nikolaevsk, rumours were flying about a bear that had recently killed two men somewhere outside the city. We went for a walk one day and, after spending a happy half-hour mushroom hunting among the birches, found out that this was precisely the place the bear had last been seen. We bundled into the car and headed back to town. But on the way we picked up a woman who said that the bear had been shot. This was not the end of talk about the bear, however, and I owe that animal a debt of gratitude for all that I learned through conversations that he started.

It happened like this. We dropped in on Rima's mother's sister while waiting for the boat back to the mainland. We told her about the bear and the interesting fact that he had passed up two women and attacked only men. "Smart bear," said Rima's mother – and who can blame her? What she meant, though, was that the bear knew that it was a man who had attacked him. Bears are being hunted for their gall-bladders, which bring a high price in Korea.

As we sat in the darkening afternoon, Maria Semyonovna told about the traditional belief that twins and their mother turn into bears after death. Twins hold a special place in Nivkh mythology and are frequently represented on a shaman's costume. They are given a special burial, she said, seated at the base of a tree.[5]

Dance from the Nivkh bear ceremony, Sakhalin Island.
(Photo by Murray Pleasance.)

67

Maria Semyonovna usually joked about everything but she was serious about this. As twins turn into bears, she said, so shamans turn into eagles. "My aunt turned into an eagle – everybody saw it flying over the house after her funeral. Children turn into birds[6] and other people into various animals and birds, including ravens. When people died, they were buried after three days. Three days after that, or four if it was a woman, people would go to the grave with tea and tobacco. They made a little fire and sat for a while. After a last ceremony at six months, we never went near the grave again."

On the other hand, Nadia said, the Udegei people go to the graves of their relatives every year. They make a fire and chat there a while. This contrasted with what Valentina Kyalundzyuga had told me the week before – that her family never visited the graves of the dead.

But we hadn't finished with the shaman-"aunt." "As a child this person was a girl," said Maria Semyonovna, "then as a youth she was male. For most of her life she was a woman, a powerful shaman. In 1937 she was sent to prison along with most of the other shamans, who were considered to be enemies of the people. When she died some time later, her body was found to be that of a man!"

I was stunned. I'd read about shamans changing sex, but this was the first time I'd met someone who knew such a person or even told a story about it.[7] Rima's mother was nodding and saying that she too knew such a person.

Then Nadia countered with memories of a woman she knew in school who was known as "it" because of the way she dressed. More stories followed that were clearly about lesbianism and cross-dressing. These topics were fairly taboo in Russia, but certainly not on a par with spontaneous sex-change. We had crossed the line back into the more commonplace. I was not the only one who had a hard time dealing with the shaman story – which seems impossible to a person with a Western rationalist upbringing. The younger generation of indigenous people also balk at such stories. Outsiders find metaphorical explanations, while insiders of the older generations accept them as literal truth. But at the time we shied away from discussing this question, tempering the astonishing with a return to the familiar, and soon boarded the boat back to the mainland.

Reflecting more deeply, this is a question that lies at the very heart of the storyteller's art and the researcher's work. On what level do these seemingly impossible things happen? Children often ask wide-eyed, "Is that a *true* story?" When I say that stories are true in the way that dreams are true, small children nod wisely, while many scholars continue to object, holding that this tale of sex-change is like an urban legend.

Researchers who are open to experience in a culture different from their own often find themselves looking with new eyes, accepting a different plane of reality. As time passes, new ideas become more widely accepted, in spite of the difficulty of translating them to a different culture. Many of us, however, remain somewhere in the middle, both accepting and questioning.

I think back to my conversations with Valentina Kyalundzyuga about the levels of protection provided by traditional clothing. She insisted that the clothing protected the girl from the winds on the ice mountain in a practical sense, while I had been thinking metaphorically. At last I realized that in her view the practical and the spiritual are not as far apart as they are in my own, and that we do not need to worry about defining boundaries so rigidly. The spirit of the wind is in the physical wind, and its chill is no metaphor.

This is the case in other areas as well. For instance, most indigenous Siberian languages do not have words for altered states of consciousness – a subject of tremendous interest to Western researchers on shamanism. To the indigenous shaman, consciousness is more of a continuum. The important thing is not the state of consciousness but the task to be accomplished. These tasks may take a shaman beyond the realm of what Westerners consider normal consciousness, but that consciousness is not considered abnormal or "altered" by the shamans themselves.

In the same way, what happens in stories may seem to be literally impossible but determining the level of reality of an event is not the point of the story. As we will see in conversations about whether or not Ul'chi shaman Anga really married a tiger (her story is told in chapter 6), the very idea of examining how "real" such events are is considered spiritually dangerous.

4

Nanai Storytelling in Dada and Jari

Nadia and I spent the third part of the month in the Nanai region, in villages on the banks of the Amur. Our driver was Leonid Maktuvich Beldi, a dairy farmer. He was very proud of his Toyota four-wheel-drive truck and never left it unattended. At his home in the village of Dada I was amazed to learn that his wife, Galia, is the sister of my old friend Nina Beldi from Sakhalin Island. I met Nina in Whitehorse in 1992 and now proudly wear her magnificently embroidered dress for storytelling performances. While most Nanai live on the mainland, Nina and her husband had moved to the island to work in the 1940s and had been there ever since.

"My sister Nina is the artist in the family," said Galia. She herself was a person who kept track of all the details. She was also immensely proud of the fact that her three children and numerous grandchildren had all turned out to be

Leonid Maktuvich Beldi with his morning's catch, Dada.

intelligent, responsible people. And that her husband didn't drink.

Galia said that dairy farming was not worth the trouble. They had twenty-three cows, were up before dawn, and never had a day off. Indeed, this was the first home I'd stayed in where I was allowed to help peel potatoes. The Beldi household was truly busy all the time.

Leonid was growing hay for their cows on a small island in the river. If he were to sell the hay, he would make more money than they did selling the milk. "Mmm," I said, gorging myself on the delicious cottage cheese and sour cream.

The other problem with keeping cows was that they were not fenced in. Leonid said that thirty or more cows were deliberately hit every year by motorists, who stole the meat. The whole investment could be gone in a moment.

Leonid went out fishing every morning. They dried fish for themselves and their family and he also used fish for barter. On our travels we made side trips to drop off fish to people who had done Leonid favours, and he used a large fish to pay the man who repaired the brakes on the Toyota before our return to the city.

The Beldis lived in a comfortable house they had built themselves on the bank of one of the tributaries of the Amur. (It is important to live on the tributaries, since the Amur itself is so polluted.) They had room for their garden and all the animals and grandchildren, and the place was easy to heat with a Russian-style brick wood stove. But they complained about not being able to get an apartment, with indoor plumbing. The thing that really bothered them was the fact that government workers who got the apartments and relatively decent salaries were not working nearly as hard as they were. "And those lazy people have houses *and* apartments." Leonid truly believed that each person's labour should have equal value. He and Galia didn't mind the work – they resented not being able to make ends meet by doing it. Leonid was proud of doing an important job and angry at seeing the communist ideal being shown as a lie. He spoke passionately. He's right, I thought, reflecting on the fact that the ideal of equality was no better realized under one political system than another.

I couldn't agree about the tigers though. Leonid thought there were too many tigers, in spite of the fact that some scientists tell us the Siberian tiger is seriously endangered, with only somewhere between twenty to three hundred left (*National Geographic*, 191, no. 2 (1997): 100–9). He deplored the number of other animals killed by the tiger in the same way he deplored the cutting of the forests that has destroyed their habitat and contributed to the declining numbers of animals and fish. Twice he had inadvertently caught tigers in his bear traps, but apart from that he said he had never seen a tiger. None of the other indigenous people I asked on this first trip had ever seen a tiger. The only other person who claimed to have seen one was a city person, a Russian on holiday in the taiga, a person I thought prone to exaggerate. Tigers don't show themselves unless they are ill or threatened. The fact that people have seen them more

frequently in the years since my conversation with Leonid
suggests that their habitat is even more severely threatened.
In 1999 Valentina Kyalundzyuga showed me the marks where
a tiger had scratched his claws on a tree in the middle of her
village.

Although Leonid has lived in the area all his life, he saw
the ancient petroglyphs at Sikachi Alyan, a few kilometres
from his home, for the first time with me. The petroglyphs,
extremely well-preserved, have been dated by archaeolo-
gists as going back 5,000 years and show images of animals
such as moose, birds, spirals, and shaman's masks that are
similar to those embroidered on clothing today.

Leonid built his house on what turned out to be a burial
site – as he began to excavate he found human bones and
silver jewellery. People were buried there after a smallpox
epidemic, the elders said. They told Leonid he should take
the bones and jewellery to the taiga and rebury them, and
so he did.

Leonid and Galia's neighbour Maria Grigorievna told
me about frog and mouse, who have endless adventures in
Nanai tales. They are the main characters in teaching tales
about generosity and greed, cleverness and persistence. Her
telling was animated, and her grandson fascinated. The
Nanai-language version was full of gestures and sounds –
the scraping of the oars, the arguments of the animals. Her
translation had only the bare bones.

FROG AND MOUSE

Frog and mouse lived together. One day mouse said,
"Let's go over to the other side of the river. The bird-cher-
ries are ripe – we'll pick some!"

They got into the boat. Mouse couldn't row, so frog
rowed them across. When they got there, mouse scam-
pered up a tree. She started to pick cherries and eat them.

Nanai men's hunting apparel by Olga Beldi.

"Throw some down for me," called frog, who couldn't climb trees.

Mouse threw down just a few cherries, and continued to eat and stuff herself.

Finally, when she was completely full, mouse came back down.

"Where are my cherries?" asked frog.

"There weren't enough for you," mouse replied.

They got back in the boat and again frog rowed. ▼

As time passed I heard a lot of variants on this tale: in one, mouse was so full that her stomach burst.[1] In another the two got back and frog was so offended that he left home. Another day they picked another kind of berry and frog was successful, mouse not. Mouse found a barn full of good food and started robbing; frog told the owner and mouse died. The cherries were green and mouse got sick. They both ate, frog's red belly stuck out. They went out for firewood, mouse got better prepared and spent the winter better. One teller points out that mice have been stealing ever since.[2]

Maria Grigorievna's mother looked out from the bedroom but didn't join us. She was one hundred years old that year. The house was full of her embroidery, including one Nanai robe embroidered in Ukrainian style, which she had done in a contest with a Ukrainian woman.

Maria Grigorievna went on with two other stories, before the demands of baby-sitting took her away. Clearly this one is about a different frog! In the folklore of the Amur region a poor housekeeper or an unpleasant woman is often called a frog.

THE TERRIBLE FROG

There was a big terrible frog. She said to one old man, "Throw your wife out and we'll live together. I'll be beautiful, I'll sew for you."

The old man softened and agreed. He didn't talk to his old woman any more. One day he went fishing and she started to clean up the house. "Oh my goodness, look at this big frog in the house! It must be your fault he's stopped talking to me," she said. "I'm going to teach you a lesson!"

She took her pipe and a stick and got out the nicotine and spread it on the frog's eyes and nose. The frog cried,

"Oh, how it hurts!"

The old man came home and guessed what his wife had done. He started to beat his wife and threw her into a hole. She turned into a duck and flew away. Her two children were crying.

The boy said, "Let's go to the beach and cry there. Maybe mama will come." So they did, and the duck came and flew around them. She flew and flew and then turned into their mother.

"If your father catches me, he'll beat me to death," she said. "Don't tell him you saw me."

She washed all their things out, and they shone like gold. "Tell him you saw the neighbour woman washing," she said, and flew away. The son understood and wanted his father and mother to make up. The daughter didn't understand. The son told his father what had happened.

The father said, "I want to make up with her. When you see your mother again, tell her to let you look for lice on her head. When she lies down, tie her hair and give me a sign."

The boy did what his father said. Then he called his father. The mother tried to raise her head but she was tied down.

The father tried to get her to forgive him. And at last she did and they lived long after that. ▾

As in many Amur tales, a child brings about reconciliation. The husband regains control of his first wife's soul through her hair. The story introduces the theme of the difficulty of a second wife entering the home, this time an ugly one, while in the next story the second wife is beautiful.

This next story may or may not be a continuation of the last. Amur tales are characteristically independent but at the same time character, plot, and meaning interconnect constantly. This one again shows the power of embroidered clothing. Much like a shaman, the hero uses it to bring a woman to life.

Detail of Nanai embroidery done by Olga Beldi.

THE GIRL IN THE ICE

They lived peacefully. But then the wife started to notice that her husband was bringing back only a little meat from the hunt and little fur.

She became jealous. She decided to follow him. She quickly braided her two women's braids into one man's braid. She got dressed, put on her skis and followed him. She came to a house and looked in. It was clean as could be, with meat on the table, but nobody was there.

78

She followed him every day and at last on the third day she looked at the crack in the ice where people stored their fish and a girl came out, so beautiful! The woman couldn't help herself, she took out her spear and stabbed the girl. The water turned red with blood and the girl disappeared. The wife quickly went home, rebraided her hair, and sat down to her embroidery.

Her husband came back and she fed him. Then his brother arrived and told what had happened, the ski tracks he had seen in the snow.

The wife said, "No it wasn't me. I didn't go anywhere. How could I?"

The husband was upset and cried. He went away to that house. A women came out and said, "My younger sister is dying and it's your fault."

"Don't blame me," he said.

"Maybe you can find her in time," she said.

So he went on. He came to a second house, and there he heard that she had passed that way, but that she was dying.

At last he came to a Nanai village. There she was lying dead. People were grieving.

"How can I live without her?" he thought.

He woke her up by placing an embroidered glove on her body. "Oh how long I've slept," she said as she awakened. "I know that your wife did this to me."

And it all came out well. When they got back the wife begged forgiveness for her envy and bad character. ▼

Like the Udegei story of Yegdyga and the seal, this one shows some of the difficulty of polygamous marriages and also relates the second wife to a water creature, with her beauty and ability to create and sustain life. The first wife was expected to accept the second, and this wife's reaction, even today, is interpreted as "envy and bad character." In 1995 I heard a third tale similar to this from Ul'chi teller Anna Kavda.[3]

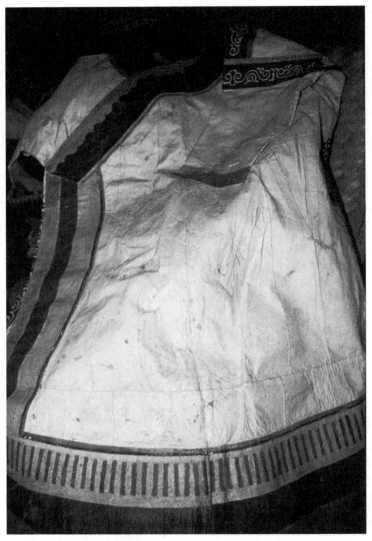

Nanai coat of salmon skin in the Troitskoe museum. Skins were
traditionally dried and softened to make an excellent wind
and waterproof material. This labour-intensive process is rarely
done today.

In Troitskoe, the next village down the river, I met Anna Petrovna Khodzher, who was director of the local museum. Under the Soviets, museums were created in most villages and towns of any size. Even Gvasyugi has a museum in one room of the school. Often though, the most valuable objects made their way to museums in Moscow and St Petersburg, and today some local people are trying to get them back. This situation is made even more problematical by the fact that both local and federal museums are severely under-funded and are having a hard time maintaining their holdings in good condition. Local museum exhibits include local flora and fauna as well as art and traditional clothing and utensils that have been donated or sold to the museum by local people. In addition to her work at the museum, Anna Khodzher is a poet and teller of tales. "I grew up in a big family with ten children," she said. "To entertain the children in the evenings, our parents played games with us and told us stories, legends, and proverbs. We guessed riddles. I grew up among the heroes of tales. My mother knew many stories because she was a great shaman. She taught me to tell them correctly, insisting that I tell them over until I remembered all the details – the names, the order of events. She showed me where to imitate the hero's intonation and things like that. She taught us to speak tongue-twisters fast and correctly. They used to say that a person who refused to tell stories would have bad luck hunting, but that tradition is gone now.

"Children were not allowed to play at night, but we loved to listen to our parents tell stories. I would get emotionally involved and often cried, but I still wanted to listen. Some of the stories had lessons in them. Some were legends and others were epics, very long. I remembered what I had heard and now I tell the stories in the evenings to my grandchildren and to children at the school."

Among the Nanai, women told stories all day and night while the hunters were away. They believed in the magic of words. Legends, *telungu*, were told only indoors, at night.

Ningman, magic-tales, were told while out fishing, hunting
or berry-picking. The Tungus words *ningma* (tale) and *ning-
machi* (funeral) have the same root, which has to do with seeing with the eyes closed (Avrorin 1986: 14–15). They show
the connection between storytelling, funerals, and shamanism: all maintain the connection with the souls of ancestors.

The next two tales are *ningman.* Just as the Udegei tales
have Yegdyga and Belye as their hero and heroine, the
Nanai have Mergen the archer as hero and Pudi or Pudin
(sometimes called Fudin) as heroine.

ENDOHOCHEN

Two sisters lived together. They did everything together,
they hunted and fished and brought in firewood and
berries.

One day one of them said, "Why are we doing everything together? Let's one of us go out to work and the
other one stay home and get food ready. Then the next
day we'll do the opposite."

And so they agreed.

The first day the younger sister went out for cranber-
ries, but she couldn't find a good spot. At last she came to
a place where there were many. She started picking them
and suddenly an arrow fell beside her and spoke in a
human voice. "Sister, go away quickly. Soon Endohochen
will come – he's half man and half dog. Run!"

She ran away in terror and told her sister about it. Her
sister listened with no reaction.

The next day the older sister went out. The younger
warned her to be careful.

She started picking berries and an arrow fell at her feet
and spoke in a human voice. "Sister, run away, Endohochen is coming and it'll be bad for you!" She paid no
attention. Sure enough pretty soon Endohochen came up

to her – he was half man and half dog.

"Let me take a look at your head," he said.

"You won't find anything," she replied, "I just washed and combed my hair."

"I'll look anyway."

He insisted so strongly that at last she agreed. He started looking for lice on her head. He pulled one out from the side of her head; it was gold on the back.

"I'll put this on your tongue."

"No, put it on the ground."

"The ground won't hold it."

"Then put it on a stone."

"The stone won't hold it."

"Then throw it out."

"No, I will put it on your tongue."

"How can my tongue hold it if the earth and the stone can't?"

"It will hold it."

And so she stuck out her tongue. Endohochen reached in and pulled out her tongue and her lungs and ran away. She ran home bleeding.

Her sister guessed what had happened. She went outside and pulled out the tongue of a puppy. She attached it to her sister's mouth using her own saliva. The older sister told the whole story in the dog's language and the younger sister understood.

"I warned you. But now this is the way we must live."

And so they went to sleep.

The older sister dreamed that an old woman appeared and said, "Go and get your own tongue. I'll leave you a white horse to help you. Go where the horse takes you. Don't tie him to a tree, but only to shrubs or wormwood. I'll leave you three bronze lizard-amulets, long ones. They will help you too." And the old woman disappeared.

When the girl woke up, there was no little old woman, but she saw the three brass lizards. She went outside and found a white horse tied to some shrubs. She got dressed

83

and took needles and a comb in her sewing bag. She said goodbye to her sister, got on the horse, and flew away. After some time she saw a big house and came down to earth beside it.

She knew what to do. She went inside and the place was full of Endohochens, including the one who had stolen her tongue. She went inside and started the fire. She brought water, added grain, and gave it to them in cups. On their plates she saw many human tongues, including her own which was still fresh.

She poured food for the old people. They were thinking she was a wonderful bride. And then she said to them, "I'm going to clean up in here. Go outside, otherwise dust will fall on your food." And so they went out, all the while thinking what a good bride she was.

As soon as she was alone, she quickly pulled out her dog's tongue and replaced it with her own. Then she gathered up the garbage and went outside.

"Go back inside. I'm just going to dump this and I'll be right back."

"What a fine bride she is!" they thought and went back in.

She got on the horse and tried to fly away. But Endohochen was holding the horse's tail. She took out her knife and cut off the tail. Away they flew.

"Where shall we go?" called the horse. "To people, or to a place where there are no people?"

"I am a person. We will go to people."

And so they flew to a settlement. The horse came down beside a small house and she tied him to some shrubs. An old man and woman lived there. "Where have you come from?" they asked. "How did you get here?"

"Endohochen is chasing me. I came here to rest."

"Stay with us, then."

Soon their son Mergen came in. The young people liked each other and after a while they got married.

Then one day he wanted to go hunting. "Let me take your horse."

"No," she said. "I need the horse. What if Endohochen comes after me?"

But he convinced her to let him take the horse. She warned him only to tie the horse to shrubs or wormwood and never to a tree, and away he went.

After he left she gave birth to a baby boy. The grandparents were very happy. The old man sent a worker to find Mergen with the news. But on the way the worker met Endohochen. And told him the news.

"I'll be seeing him," said Endohochen. "I'll tell him. You go back and give them this message, 'That which you find outdoors, throw it away. And the thing that is off to the side, you don't need. Throw it away.'"

And the worker went back and gave the message.

Pudin wept.

She could tell that Endohochen was coming.

She made a carrying bag and put her son on her back. If only the horse were there! How could she get away? She started to run. Already she could see Endohochen approaching.

She reached in her sewing bag and threw out her needle. "Turn into a thick forest!"

And a thick forest sprung up behind her. Endohochen got lost in it. She stopped to rest and fed the baby. And she called out to her horse, "Horse, wherever you are, hear my voice and come to help me!"

And then she heard Endohochen getting close. She ran on. This time he almost caught her. But she threw out the comb. And it too turned into a thick forest. She didn't hear Endohochen any more so she stopped for a rest and fed the baby. And she called to the horse, "Give me strength!"

And then she heard Endohochen again. She ran on, feeling more rested now. And then she remembered the three bronze lizards. She threw them out and they became three pillars. She climbed up to the top of one of them and sat there feeding the baby. Endohochen came up and started to chew on the pillar she was sitting on. He broke his teeth, and blood poured from his mouth, but he kept on chewing.

The pillar was about to fall. She jumped over to the next pillar. He chewed more slowly this time, but nonetheless before long the pillar was rocking, about to topple over. She jumped to the third pillar. Still Endohochen was chewing away at the bronze. And finally this too was about to fall.

And then in the distance she saw it. The size of a mosquito at first, then getting closer and closer. Yes! It was the horse!

"Fly faster!" she called.

She could see that the horse was pulling a tree stump behind him. But he got there. She jumped on, cut the rope to the stump with her knife and they flew away.

"Where will we go?" called the horse. "To people or to a place where there are no people?"

"Experience speaks. We will go to a place where there are no people."

And so they went to a good place. And the horse told her what had happened.

"Your husband tied me to a tree stump. I heard you calling and tried and tried to tear loose. I had to use so much energy just getting free that I barely arrived in time. And now I am dying. Don't cry. When I die, take off my skin and wrap yourself in it. I have helped you as much as I can."

And the horse died.

She wept and then removed the skin with her knife. She wrapped herself and the baby in it and they slept a long time.

When she woke up she saw that she was in a big fine house. The sun was shining in the window and all the clothes were clean. Meat was cooking over a good fire and wood was piled beside the hearth. And on one of the sleeping benches, two baby moose were playing. She was happy as she sat up and looked at all this.

Her baby boy grew fast. In five days he was bringing back rabbit and in nine days ducks. But then one day he came running home out of breath.

"Endohochen is coming!"

She picked up the child and got ready to run. But it was too late. She didn't know what to do so she just sat down. But then she caught sight of the baby moose. Just then Endohochen ran in. She guessed what to do. She cut the moose babies free and they fought long and hard with Endohochen. And they killed him.

She was very happy. She pulled the evil thing outside and burned it.

And so they lived.

One day the boy came in calling, "Father's coming!"

She tied the door shut. But the boy opened it. He was happy to meet his father. But she was angry. "Why did you tie my horse to a tree when I told you not to?"

"It's not my fault," he said. "I forgot."

"I will not go back with you."

And so they argued. But at last she forgave him. They all began living together.

Then one morning they noticed that the moose babies were gloomy, while normally they were cheerful. "What's the matter?" she asked. "Have we taken bad care of you?"

"We were sent by the heavenly god to help you when you were having a hard time with those evil spirits. But now that is past and it is time for us to go."

They all wept and embraced. She cooked kasha and sewed special silk clothes as gifts of thanks. They bowed low, thanking the moose for their help. The two moose flew up to heaven, still looking back and bowing. At last they disappeared. The time had come.

She cooked more kasha and made offerings. And then they looked around. The house was gone. Everything looked as if nobody had ever lived there. And so they went back to her husband's parents. When they got there the old people were arguing, each one blaming the other.

Mergen said, "Don't argue. It was all the fault of the evil spirits." And so they all lived together. ▼

"Endohochen" begins with the same images of the lice and the stolen tongue as Eofu Kimonko's story of the two sisters in chapter 1. Here it is developed considerably further and includes the heavenly moose who appear in Sikachi-Alyan petroglyphs, as well as the heroine's horse. Since horses are relatively recent newcomers to the Amur region, having arrived with the Russion settlers, it is safe to assume that the horse must have entered the story either very recently, after Russian contact, or a long time ago. I think it is possible he came with the Tungus peoples on their long journey from central Asia, where horses are the most vital companions a person can have. This horse acts very much like horses belonging to epic heroines among the Turks and Mongols in giving good advice, rescuing the girl in time of trouble, and at last transforming his body into a comfortable house. This last transformation brings to mind the house built of bear bones in Dusia Kimonko's story "Sister and Brother."[4] And, like Dusia's heroines in "Two Sisters," this heroine burns the evil creature in the end. The way Endohochen intercepts the message to the husband is reminiscent of the European tale of the "Handless Maiden," a version of which I have heard told in Tuva – another connection to the Turkic world.

The girl in this story may be going through a kind of shamanic initiation, helped in her meeting with the evil spirits by the old woman, her horse, the moose babies, her comb, and her sewing tools. As a man is helped by his spear and arrows, the woman is helped by her needles, knives, and sharpening stones. In this story throwing the needle recalls protective power of embroidered images. Lizard amulets are representations of shamanic helping spirits and here they turn into pillars, which resemble the poles that shamans of the past kept outside their houses.

In the next story a boy learns how to be a good hunter

and the importance of obeying tradition. But, like the heroine in "Endohochen," his disobedience leads to a transfor-
mative meeting with evil spirits.

THE BOY WHO WENT TO A FORBIDDEN PLACE

A young boy lived with his mother.

"When you play outside you must only go upriver, never
down."

He grew up and obeyed her. But one day he thought,
"Why does she say that? I'll go down the river and see
what's there."

He went down the river and came to a big house. He
went in and there on the *nakan*, the sleeping bench, was a
huge frog. He killed the frog and went home.

"Why did you tell me not to go downstream?" he asked
his mother. And he told her what he had done.

"Why did you kill the frog? She was the mother of nine
evil spirits and now they will come to find you."

She got him ready for the road. She gave him pancakes
and fishcakes. "You must run away," she told him.

As soon as he left the door opened. In came the nine
evil spirits. "Where is your son?" they asked.

"I have no son."

"You lie. Where is he? He killed our mother." And they
began to tickle her. Just before she lost consciousness, she
pronounced the word, "Island Bor."

They left her there.

When she came to, she wept. Then she swept the floor
and found one of the boy's buttons. She swallowed it and
became pregnant. She bore a second son. He grew quickly, in five days he got a rabbit and in nine days a duck.

As he grew older he began to ask, "Mama, do I have a
brother?"

"No."

"Why are there children's toys here?"

She still said he had no brother.

The boy grew up and started to go out in his *omorochka*, his little boat. One day he came to the Island Bor. He heard a sound, "Kopya kopya kopya kopya. My heart and all my insides are dried up. They make this sound like bells, kopya kopya kopya kopya."

He saw a boy running around and around the island. Nine evil spirits were running after him, around and around.

The boy thought, "How can I save him?"

He shot one arrow, aiming so that it went through all nine evil spirits. But still the boy kept running around and around. The second brother pulled out his lasso and caught him. He was very light and still making that sound. He laid him in the boat and they went home.

The younger brother went inside and said to his mother, "I got a rabbit. Go outside and get it."

She went outside and she too heard that sound and the song. She rushed over and picked her son up. She brought him inside and fed him rabbit and blueberries. She washed him and cared for him and he got well.

And from then on he never again disobeyed the traditions. ▼

Women are central to tradition, like the boy's mother who could do everything. But I had read that women were forbidden to play the bowed string instruments that sound like weeping. It was thought that if they did they and their children would be unhappy. Nonetheless they often did play and according to Anna Petrovna, it was a woman who invented the instrument.[5] She wrote a poem about it, which I have translated in prose. The poet draws a parallel between a long-ago epidemic and destructive events of the Soviet period, affirming her belief that music can bring a dying culture to life.

DUCHIEKE[6]

Long ago on the earth there was no one yet who could tell
it all correctly. My great-grandfather's great-grandfather
heard from his great-grandfather that once, out of the
south-eastern mountains, a black cloud came gloomily
crawling, bringing an unseen pestilence to the banks of
the Amur. Neither amulets nor roots and grasses could
help anyone. Even the animals ran away from the black
horror of this infection. The shaman, whose soul was not
blind although the way of the healer was filled with difficulty, rang his shaman's belt in impotent rage. Into the
fire he threw his drum, which had gone silent.

They died one after the other, the people of that village
where they had once been happy. And over the plain rose
acrid smoke and a numberless crowd of fat flies. Once,
like a wounded beast on the path, like a spirit from *Buni*,
like the product of imagination, a woman crawled from an
earth hut. The fires were still smoking when, waking for a
short time, she realized that she could defeat the black
death, which had destroyed the tribe. But why, if the world
is kind, why did the clan die? Not a seed, not an ear of any
grain left. Not even graves were left. No human voice was
to be heard.

I do not know what her mother called her heart, in the
night. But I know for certain that she was my foremother
and sister. Again it seems that it is I who wander in the
taiga gripped in the vice of loneliness. My soul languishes
and I do not want to live in the wide world. I wish that a
bear would take me, or a wolf hiding behind a fir tree. I
want to die, die, die. To return forever to my people! But I
have no strength, and it is not known for how long I must
suffer in impotence and rage.

And suddenly under my heart – a jolt, another! Life has
awakened in this tortured womb! And suddenly I remem-

ber that night. The moon came shining through the needles of the cedar and you whispered to me, "Let there be
a daughter." I answered, "I will bear you a son." But whom
will I bring him to now? Who will educate him to his man-
hood, teach him to follow tracks in the forest, to shoot
from the bow, and all the wisdom that goes with this?
"Search for people," whisper the branches. "Search ..."
echoed on the quiet pools. Of course the branch was
right. But who will tell me where to find them? Shall I
shout? But my voice disappeared long ago. It went with my
tears into the dry loam. The autumn forest is dark and
cold. From age-old cedars to blades of grass. I don't know
what news, whose wisdom and whose great power told me
that there was a way out, and enlightened me with this
true thought.

There is flexible willow, there is birch-bark and fish-skin
prepared by my mother's hand. And the idea is simple! If
only I can do it, if only it will work out. But the heart
knows what it is doing, and woman's fingers are so obedi-
ent ... The violin doesn't speak yet – I must dream up its
string voice. My hair went grey in my trouble, it grew cold
in the icy water, the wind dried it like the blade of a knife.
Now my hair will become live strings. Clean, like the flow
of the river, weep like my soul, *duchieke!* Down along the
current, my soul, up along the current, my soul. Carry my
open heart, my suffering with the voice of your strings.
May the play of the early morning waves answer her, my
soul. And flow together with her, my soul. I have cried out
all my eyes – only your string is left that the forest may
hear me, that I may express all my grief.

At my wedding I danced as no one has danced in a century. But suddenly darkness covered the sun, and there is
no joy left, my soul. Sound, string, to a hundred versts.[7]
May the nine stars of my hope burst in the thunderous
realms through the nine guarding clouds. Like sprouts of
the willow, the love that I carry in my heart, you, my soul,
have resurrected my people from the darkness of ages.

This was long ago, and grandfather Kolbo the wood-carver now holds in his hand a Nanai violin, *duchieke*, which attracts no one. Young people walk by with tape recorders. He looks after them – who knows if it is truth or lies that fly from their tight cassettes? He takes up the duchieke and lifts the wing of the bow, and again there are tears on my cheek and the centuries part. As if I am wandering again in the empty taiga, with the Amur before me. Again I am making a duchieke from birch-bark and fish-skin. Not to sweeten your hearing without memory or care. But to resurrect my ancient clan, killed by the pestilence. ▼

Anna Petrovna talked about poetry, about needing the time and the mood to write. She had published one volume of verse but now she had neither the time nor the mood to write more. (Since 1993, she has retired and returned to writing.) Her job and her family made it difficult to concentrate on poetry. I thought longingly of my own musical instruments, so like the one in the story, that I had left behind to come here, and about the creative spirit.

5

Nanai Storytelling in Nergen and Naikhin

The village of Nergen lies at the end of a long bad road. But the reward is a charming place on a hill beside the river. People there grow gardens, fish, and walk to the central well with buckets slung over their shoulders on poles. Village children bring to school archaeological finds that they have dug up in the garden – in Soviet times, when wearing Nanai clothing was forbidden, people hid their jewellery in the garden and sometimes forgot where it was buried.

We stayed with Violetta Khodzher and her mother. Violetta had started a society that employed local people in ecologically sensitive logging and construction. They also had a small store. "We're trying to find a way for our men to work without breaking their backs. But we need a bit of equipment. It's hard to know which way to turn with the economy so bad."

Violetta was unusual among young women of the area in

Salmon drying at the home of Violetta Khodzher, Upper Nergen.

being unmarried. Her drive and initiative are also exceptional, but she comes from a line of strong women. They rarely even talk about men, except in long recitations of who married whom. The men seem to fish and drink, while the women move ahead.

On the way back from the *banya* (Russian bath) Violetta told me several legends, standing in the road under a starry sky. These are distinguished from magic tales in that they are about events that happened within the memory of the people Violetta heard them from.

VIOLETTA'S LEGENDS

There used to be an island in the middle of the river. It was formed from the body of a girl who was turned to stone on her way to her wedding. The island had the form of a girl with all her things. No one lived on the island, but people used to go there to be healed. There was a certain hole in the rock. If you could go through the hole you would live – if not, you would die. We found round stones there with holes in the middle. They weren't common, and when I found them I'd put them in my pocket. But my mother made me put them back. "You must not take anything from that island," she said. It was a sacred place. The Soviets took stone away from the island to use for building, and it has now disappeared.

There once was a shaman who said, "When I die, take me to a place where there are no people. And don't come back for three days and three nights. I will come back to life." Well, of course some people couldn't resist – they came close on the first night and heard the sound of a faraway drum. The second night the sound was closer. The third night one of them coughed and they all ran away. The next day they came and saw the body of the shaman

96

on his hands and knees. He had almost come back to life.

In the Tsar's time the governor invited the shaman from the village of Naikhin to the city of Khabarovsk. The shaman showed the governor what he could do. The governor watched in amazement and then asked for more. "All right," said the shaman, "if you really want more I can turn you into a bear!" The governor declined and sent the shaman home loaded with rewards. ▼

There was one shaman in Nergen in 1993 – Olga Grigorievna Beldi. She was busy embroidering seven new dresses for her own funeral, which she calmly said was not far away. On the way to the next world she may use the dresses to pay the spirits and ensure her arrival in the land of her ancestors.

A friend from the city of Amursk was visiting Olga Grigorievna. Her name is Tomto Vasilievna Beldi and she was born in 1915. She told this story, which was translated from Nanai to Russian on the spot by Anna Khodzher.

THE MOSQUITO NET

Pudin lived alone, without even knowing that her brother and his wife lived nearby. She hunted and fished and brought in all her own firewood. She wore men's clothes. She got moose and all kinds of food, bear, boar, and furs too. She was also a fine artist.

One day out in the taiga something fell beside her. It was a silk mosquito net. It tore the hem of her dress. She was angry and tore the mosquito net. Blood came from it.

She was afraid. She went home and sat up all night beside the fire. Before long a woman came to see her. It was her brother's wife.

"You are very guilty," she said. "You have almost killed

Historic Nanai dress. Collection of Violetta Khodzher, Nergen.

someone. Your brother has gone to try to put things right.
You must go to this man and work for him and marry
him." And so they started moving her things to her brother's place. Servants worked day and night loading things
into a big boat with ten pairs of oars.

Pudin came to the village where this Mergen lived. As
she stepped from the boat there was nobody to be seen.
Her brother and his wife went into the village and didn't
come back. She walked along the walkway-bridge.

A Manchurian woman came and dropped her shoes
over the edge and blamed Pudin. A second woman
appeared, dropped her long pipe, and blamed Pudin. A
third woman came and she was a kind one. She
approached and invited them to come in. Servants carried
her things. They cooked their own food. Pudin came in

98

and saw a man under a mosquito cover. He was injured. Her brother was trying to make peace but the man didn't answer. At night the man called to her to bring him water. "If you are a good woman, bring me water."

She brought it and he threw it in her face. Next he called for his pipe. She brought it and he threw that too.

The next morning her brother asked where she got the lump on her head and she said from bumping the door handle. But her brother wasn't sleeping and he knew.

The brother went away leaving people to look after her. He told Mergen not to kill his sister.

Mergen decided to go hunting. All his wives set out to sew something for him. Pudin said, "I can't, I don't know how to do anything."

She quickly cut something out and put it under her pillow. Next day the other wives complained they hadn't had time to do anything. Pudin still said she couldn't sew or embroider but she pulled her designs from under the pillow and they were magnificent. The other wives hadn't done anything.

The next time Mergen went hunting he brought the best parts to her, and her brother also brought her things. Again Mergen hunted and brought meat and the third time he went to a Manchurian town and brought wonderful things; cloth, threads, food, candy.

Mergen came in and Pudin threw out her long hair. He gathered it up, coming toward her, and they made their peace. At first she was offended but at last they made up.

And then they had the wedding. ▼

The brother knowingly marries his sister to an abusive man, negotiating with him for her well-being. It's possible that the incident with the mosquito net is a prophetic dream. Anna Petrovna drew the moral that Pudin eventaully won because of her hard work, beauty, and silence, showing the way a woman could survive in such circumstances. In shamanic terms, the heroine gains control over the evil in the abusive man and transforms it, just as women today are transforming society.

Anna then told several more tales, including one about the further adventures of frog and mouse, taking up where Maria Grigorievna left off.

FROG, MOUSE, AND MOOSE

Frog and mouse have had a falling out because of the cherries and this is what happened next.

Frog was offended that mouse wouldn't share with him, and frog couldn't climb the tree. Frog goes away and finds a barn. Mice are in there fighting and stealing grain. And so he goes on and comes to a big village. There's a big house and servants running back and forth.

Frog wanted to get in and ran between the servants' legs. He saw the master sitting on the bench and jumped right into his lap.

"Where did this frog come from? Servants, throw this frog out of here."

And then frog spoke in a human voice, "Don't throw me out. I'm not that kind of frog. I saw your barn on my way, and I saw rats and mice stealing your grain."

"Servants, go and look!"

A servant went and looked and came back.

"Yes, it is true that mice and rats are stealing your grain."

"Go and get them out of there this minute! And as for this frog, feed him well, with the best food. Dress him in silk." And so frog was given kasha and all the best food, and then they dressed him in silk.

And then frog went on, jumping along. And met a moose. "Hey, moose, let's have a race!"

"What kind of competition could that be? You're nothing but a little frog and just take a look at me!"

100

"Never mind, let's just race. The one who is left behind will bleed black blood and die."

"I'm sure to beat such a little frog," thought the moose, and so he agreed. Just as soon as he started to run, frog jumped up behind his antlers. Moose ran and ran and then stopped.

"Hey froggie, where are you?" So then frog jumped down over moose's antlers onto the ground.

"What took you so long?" he said, "I've been sitting here so long waiting for you that I'm freezing to death."

"What the ... All right let's try again."

Again frog jumped onto the moose's head. And moose ran as fast as he could, huffing and puffing. And again when he stopped, frog jumped down over his antlers.

"What took you so long? I'm so cold I'm trembling."

"Can I really be so bad that a frog beat me?" And the moose was so ashamed that he bled black blood and died.

Frog went on, jumping and jumping. He came to a house, and in it there was a beautiful girl, Pudin, making embroidered designs. Her hair was lovely there on the bench beside her, like snakes. Frog watched and then jumped right onto her drawing board.

"Where did that frog come from?" she said and looked for something to throw at the frog. But then he spoke in a human voice.

"Don't kill me. Go out and look. Not far from here I killed a moose. Let's go and cut up the meat."

"What kind of a frog could have killed a moose?"

"Really, I did."

She didn't believe him but all the same at last she decided to go with him. She got ready and got the sled ready because it was winter. Frog jumped along beside her. And sure enough they came to the moose. She cut it up and brought a lot of meat home. And then she went to sleep, throwing a cloth on the floor for frog to sleep on.

She slept and then woke up. "How could I have slept so long? It's already light," she thought. And she went outside. It was dark out there, the stars were shining. What could this be? Why was it so light in the house?

She went back in. She happened to look beside the hearth and there lay Mergen, and such a Mergen! The whole house was light from his beauty. And the frog skin was lying beside him. She quietly came up to him and took the frog skin and threw it in the fire.

Mergen woke up, "What have you done? How can I live? In my childhood I was turned into a frog to protect me from evil."

"What's done is done," she said. "Now you're a man and we will live." And so they lived together.

And there's more beyond that! ▼

When Mergen no longer needed protection, Pudin burned his frog skin, the same way other heroines burned evil creatures in tales. Some heroines hide the animal skin their man has been wearing, and others simply set it aside. In one story a woman burned a skin while the man was out hunting and then watched in horror as her husband ran from the forest in flames. It seems there are greater and lesser degrees of readiness to give up that form of protection.[1]

Nadezhda Kimonko tells a story she heard from her grandmother that begins with the race between frog and moose. After winning the race, frog is thrown off onto the ice, which leads into another well-known Siberian folktale, often called "Who Is the Strongest?" The frog asks the ice if it is the strongest thing in the world and the ice says yes. The frog then sees that the sun can melt the ice, a cloud can block out the sun, the wind can disperse the cloud, and, since the winds come from the heavens, god in heaven is the strongest. Soviet versions say that the mountain blocks the cloud, a tree's roots break up the mountain, and in the end man is strongest because he can chop down the tree. But other versions of this tale go on to say that death is stronger than a man, and the shaman is stronger than death but is afraid of fire, which in turn can be put out by water. The story has then come full circle to where it began. Nadia's grandmother's version, influenced by Christianity, stops with god in heaven, and the Soviet editions stop with man. Some versions are told without an ending. Clearly the earlier versions illustrate the cyclical nature of life on earth. In a similar way the story of frog and mouse connects to the great cycle of mythic animal tales.

Anna remembers that some stories were used to teach children how to behave. Here are two of these teaching tales.

POLE, CAVIAR, BLADDER, HAYSTACK, AND BIGEYES

Before you do something you should prepare.

In one house there lived a pointed pole named *tuchun*, for hanging fish to dry, some caviar, a bladder, a haystack, and big eyes. They lived in a friendly way and one time they decided to cook some kasha.

Tuchun went out and started a big fire, poured some water in the pot, and put in enough grain to make kasha. The fire was so hot that the kasha started to boil over.

The pole called to the caviar, "Go to the barn and get some butter!" Caviar went and took bladder along. As soon as caviar went outside, along came raven and – tup – off with caviar, dragged her away. The pole was waiting for the butter and called haystack, "Go get the butter and see where those two have gone. The kasha is boiling over." As soon as haystack went outside, the wind blew so strongly that haystack was carried to the river and away. Big eyes was all that was left. He was so big that he couldn't see. He looked and looked, and pointed pole poked out the eyes by accident.

Tuchun was left alone. The kasha was burnt. He poked his own stomach, and they all died.

We heard that story and we laughed at those who couldn't do anything, who weren't prepared. ▼

Back of Nanai fishskin dress. The blue applique designs are also
of fishskin, died with berries.

THE LAZY BOY

A boy lived alone with no parents. He slept and slept and
one time he saw a dream.

Grandmother came in and said, "Why do you sleep so
much? How will you grow up? Get up! Go outside!"

He opened his eyes – there was no grandmother but he

104

started to get up. He tried to tear his head away from the pillow but it was stuck. He tried to get up but the mattress was stuck to him. He had slept so much that everything was stuck!

Still, finally he got up. He tried to open the door but couldn't. He pushed and pushed and at last a small crack appeared and he got out. And really, it was so fine out there, birds were singing merrily.

"How could I have slept so long?" he thought. He walked along, enjoying everything. And there on the hangers he saw, what was it? Something red. Fish! He reached and reached, trying to get it. But he couldn't. And at last he fell and died.

This story laughs at lazy people. ▼

Anna's last tale includes many themes now familiar, the shamanic theme of marriage with an animal, the value of the youngest and the most despised. Storytelling is shown as a way of telling uncomfortable truths in a family, as once again a child brings about a reconciliation. "Puppy" is a raccoon-dog.

THE PUPPY

A man had seven wives. Each was dearer than the other. But the one called Nalumdye was always busy.

Once the man decided to go hunting. He asked each wife, "What will you do while I am gone?"

"I'll make you a robe," said one.

"I'll make mitts," said another.

Each one had an answer, promising something.

Nalumdye says, "I'll bear you such an fascinating child that he will interest you very much!"

None of the other wives did anything. But Nalumdye gave birth to Puppy – a child not human but like a dog.

All the other wives laughed at her, saying she had slept with a dog.

The husband came back and asked what they had done. One wife says, "Oh I was so sick …" Each has a reason for doing nothing, nobody had prepared. He asks Nalumdye and she says, "Here is an interesting child."

And there on the bed sat the puppy. Of course the husband embraced and caressed the child. Nalumdye was still always busy.

Then once the elder wife seemed to get sick, very sick. The second wife spoke to the husband, "Our sister is sick, very sick. She may die. What will we do?"

"How can we heal her?" he asked.

"You must kill that Puppy and give her his blood."

Well, an order is an order, and from the elder wife, the mistress of the house …

Of course Nalumdye cried. After all, Puppy was an animal but a nice one.

Her husband went to kill the child. But instead he took a puppy from one of the servants and gave the blood to his wife. He took Puppy and went into the woods and spoke to him, "Even if you're an animal, I respect you and I won't kill you. Go and find yourself a place. If you stay at home either they will kill you or they'll make me kill you. Meanwhile I'll kill this puppy to fool them."

And so he did. He let that puppy-child go, after making him a little place to live, and left him. He took the blood back and his elder wife got better.

And the life of Puppy went on. He walked day and night and at last came to a village. There was one house off to the side and there hung a blanket. He took it and wrapped up and went to sleep.

One young woman Pudin came out and called, "Hey sister. What's going on? There's no wind but your blanket has fallen. Go bring it in."

The youngest went and picked it up. And little Puppy fell out. She wrapped him back up and took him in and threw the blanket on her own sleeping place.

"Well, well," said her older sister, "What's going on here? Why are you suddenly throwing your blanket when usually you put it away?"

"It's almost time to go to bed. What's the difference?" The time came and she lay down to sleep. Puppy was in her bed. In the morning they all got up except that Pudin.

The oldest sister said, "Why are you sleeping so late? You usually get up early."

She was silent.

Then the oldest sister said to their father, "Look at your favourite. You think she's such a hard worker but now she's just sleeping." She went up and pulled off the blanket. And Puppy was lying with her! "Look! Shame on her. Your beauty, look what she's doing! Look who she's sleeping with!"

But the father looked and he saw a handsome young man. And he said to his oldest daughter, "See, my Kharmadi, what a fine bridegroom she found!" And he was happy.

They were married. And soon a son was born to them. As in the stories, he grew fast; in five days he killed a rabbit, and in nine days a duck. Soon he was hunting all kinds of animals. And he would play and run.

One day he went far away and found a house. He went in and there were servants. The man had many wives. The boy played there.

The women said, "Who is this boy who has come in without being invited and is making all this noise and won't let anybody sleep?"

The old man said, "Quiet, let him play." And the boy played. Then it was evening and time to sleep. The old man asked, "Where do you live, far away from here?"

"No, not far," said the boy.

"Well, you can spend the night."

Every woman wanted to sleep with this boy but he refused. He also refused to sleep with the old man.

"Well, who will you sleep with?" they asked

And he pointed to one woman, the poor one. It was Nalumdye. She said, "I sleep poorly. All I have is my robe and nothing more. How will you sleep?"

"Don't worry, I'll lie beside you." And so he lay beside her. She had nothing.

The old man asked, "Can you tell a story?"

"I can."

"Well, tell us a story."

So he began to tell them their own story. About how it had all been. And when he got to the part about the lazy wives they all said, "Hey, what kind of story is this?"

The old man said, "You don't have to listen. I'll listen."

The boy went on about the puppy and the blood. Again the wives objected. And at last the boy said, "Grandfather, I am your grandson," and he ran away home and told his parents where he had been.

"Soon grandfather will come," he told them.

"How do you know you have a grandfather?"

"I know."

And in the morning the old man and Nalumdye came running. They saw this Mergen who had been Puppy. They all embraced and kissed.

This man had not valued his wife, but now he understood that he was mistaken. And he took this family home. And the other wives all hung themselves from shame. ▼

Nadia and I went on to the village of Naikhin and visited shaman Mingo Chusanbovna Geiker and her husband, Nikolai Petrovich Beldi. They were both bright-eyed and each complained loudly about the faults of the other. "He's lazy." "She's lazy." "He drinks." "She tells me what to do."

They kept their belongings strictly separate. And praised each other behind their backs.

While Nadia consulted with Mingo about the headaches Anna Dinchuevna from Gvasyugi was suffering, he reclined on the couch and told me about how dangerous fishing

Petroglyph at Sikachi Alyan on the Amur river, which may show a
shaman's mask. The petroglyphs are about 5,000 years old.

used to be on the Amur.

"Why there were so many fish jumping into your boat that you might sink! And the fish might hit you on the head and knock you out!"

I mentioned hearing that the Beldi clan was descended from the tiger.

"That's so," he said with a twinkle in his eye. "Some story about a woman marrying a tiger.

TIGER STORY

A woman was living alone and got pregnant. The man only appeared to her at night. She had two sons. When they grew up she got them well dressed one day and told them not to go out. "I'll show you your father," she said. She took them to the shore and washed them. When they came home, there on the bench lay a big tiger. "That is your father," she said. "Don't touch him." ▼

My ancestors used to go to that house all the time to make sacrifices to that tiger. Even my father and his brother went there all the time, although my father's brother was head of the local *kolkhoz*. But when I was growing up I didn't know about any of this.

"One time I went hunting with my mother's cousin. He didn't believe in anything – not shamans, not Christianity or the devil, nothing. Well, one day we were out hunting together and we saw tiger tracks. I was young, about fifteen, and thought it was a bear track. Anyway this uncle suddenly dropped down on his knees and bowed his head to the ground. I thought maybe he was sick. My eyes got big. What was the matter? I asked him why he bowed down and he said to me, 'The tiger is our ancestor. You have to bow to the tiger tracks.' Just imagine, a man who didn't believe anything else, but he believed that!"

Nikolai told a story about the powers of a famous shaman of the Passar clan. Although he told it mostly for a laugh, it contains several important shamanic themes: death and rebirth, the importance of dreams, and the way the life force is contained in a bone – in this case the shaman's finger. Like Anna Khodzher and Valentin Geiker, Nikolai connects legend with history and the idea of death and rebirth with the revival of his people.

THE PASSAR SHAMAN

A famous shaman of the Passar clan lived on one side of the river. Every day he went down to the river and sat there fishing. On the other side lived a powerful Manchu prince. The prince's daughter dreamed of the Passar shaman and got pregnant. The father was angry and questioned his daughter. "Where have you been? Who have you been with?"

"I haven't been anywhere," she replied. "But I dreamed of the Passar shaman."

The father sent soldiers across the river to kill the shaman. They cut his body in pieces with their swords.

The next morning the Manchu prince looked out and saw the shaman fishing in the river as usual, still alive.

Again he sent his soldiers. The soldiers cut the shaman up and came back and reported to the prince.

Again the next day the prince looked out and saw that the shaman was still alive, sitting beside the river fishing. He sent his soldiers again.

And so it went every day. At last the shaman got sick of it! Every day, the soldiers coming over and cutting his body into pieces! He gathered all his Passar relatives together and told them to move away from that place. "I'll stay behind," he said.

The next day the soldiers came to kill him again. This

time the prince himself came with them to find out how the shaman was reviving. "How can I kill you?" he asked.

"You'll never kill me," said the shaman. "Take me across with you."

So the prince took him over.

"If you can cut off my middle finger I will die completely," said the shaman. "But you will never find the finger."

They cut off his middle finger, but it flew away and they couldn't find it. The shaman died. The finger flew to the north of the river Sungari. All the relatives were gathered there. That finger turned into a woman shaman.

The prince went looking but all the people were gone. The soldiers rode after them, chasing them. Snow began to fall and those soldiers were in summer clothes. They turned around and came back.

The Passars went down the river to the area around Khabarovsk and Sikachi-Alyan. Just one Passar got as far as Omi, but now there are many of them there. ▼

Mingo said nobody in Naikhin bothered her about being a shaman. If people want to live, they come, she says – if not, they don't. She told us one anecdote from her life, about relations with the spirit of the forest. This spirit, called *Podya*, appears as male or female at various times and embodies the spiritual essence of a given place, its earth, trees, fire, and water. By whatever name, people all over Siberia give offerings to *Podya*, a custom that survived the Soviet period intact.

APPLESAUCE

During the war I had to go hunting. That's supposed to be a man's work, but all the men were away. When my husband came home afterward he was sick, so I kept on going hunting. One time a group of us went out. After the war some new foods came to our area and we had some apple-sauce with us. We gave *Podya* an offering of applesauce. During the night, the leader of our group saw a dream. In it *Podya* spoke to him, saying how much he liked this new flavour. And our hunting was successful. I got sixteen sables! ▼

Mingo let us watch as she did a shamanic ceremony for a woman who was in the hospital in Troitskoe. The woman had sent a bottle of vodka for the spirits and Mingo poured out a glass which she set in the corner. Then she took her drum and chanted for the woman. When she was finished she had me and Nadia take a drink of the vodka and then made it clear that the ceremony was over and we should leave.

During the year between this visit and the next I attended a workshop in Washington state given by Mingo and three helpers, Lilia and Olga Beldi and Nadezhda Duvan. Here I learned much more about Mingo, her heritage, and her practice. Mingo's shamanic lineage is in the Zaksor clan. She says they were the first Nanai shamans and are very powerful. When she described her life as a shaman, Mingo spoke in the third person.

"In the lineage of shamans, a child who will be a shaman is noted immediately at birth and grows in a special way. She resembles a crazy person. As soon as the child starts to recognize herself in this world, to see her own paths and future road, life becomes very complex. She meets not only good spirits but bad ones – *amban*. So the shaman must make her peace, come to terms with these evil spirits. On the way she meets much that is fearful." Here Mingo added details which she asked us not to repeat, saying that it is dangerous to talk widely of such matters.

The story of her inner journey reminded me of many of the magic tales I have heard. The difference between the inside and outside views of shamanic initiation is striking.

Her interior journey takes her to places both beautiful and fearful and she speaks with various beings. For instance, she described a place where shamans keep the souls they have recovered from evil spirits before returning them to a body – a kind of hospital where souls receive the care they need until they are strong enough to sustain life in a body.[2]

From the outside, however, the new shaman looks crazy. "She may run outside naked when the temperature is minus 40," said Mingo. "She may go into freezing water. No one can hold her – she kicks and bites them furiously."

Mingo spent ten years exploring these roads. At the end of this period all the shamans gathered together, the great shamans – those who accompany the dead – all the healers except those in the lowest category, those who heal only themselves.[3] Mingo wore a special hat made with wood streamers. She says that there was one special shaman at her consecration whose job it was to drive the evil spirits away from her. That older shaman caught the evil spirits and bit them, and she bit Mingo too, so hard that she passed out. Nobody touched her – she came to in her own time. When she came to herself she started to sing. The new shaman had awakened.

During her travels she had also searched for the instruments she would use as a shaman. All these things were now in the barn ready to be also consecrated. The drum (*unuchku*), the stick and belt (*yampa*). The spirit images she had found in her travels were prepared during the consecration. The wood for the rim of the drum and the skin for its top had been prepared a year in advance. The future shaman pointed out the tree to be used for the rim and her relatives went out to get it. The drum head was made from the skin of a roe deer killed in summer and the striking stick was covered with suede from the leg of a roe deer killed in winter. The glue was made from salmon. All this was ready for the day of the consecration.

The ceremony was a big, solemn, celebratory occasion. People come from villages near and far. It went on for three days – every shaman present participated in the *kamlanie,* or shamanic activity. Everybody could dance but only the shamans could drum. The feasting went on for several more days but only the people closest to the shaman stayed for the last few. Mingo added slyly that some people even fell in love at this time!

During the ceremony, *sevéns* (spirit figures) were pre-pared of wood, silver and other metal. The new shaman determined which craftsman was to cut the tree and make the *sevéns,* which are earthly representations of spirits. One test of the new shaman was that she must tell which side of the tree had been cut to get the wood. There are special rituals for empowering the drum and *sevéns.* Songs and prayers help the objects to come alive, as their spirits enter them. Mingo says that the *sevéns* should be empowered on the same day they are made.

After this the new shaman was ready to practice. Mingo worked in her village throughout the Soviet period until her death in 1997.

This was the end of my first Amur journey. But before going home I stopped back in Khabarovsk where I met one more Udegei woman, a medical doctor named Lyuba Passar. Lyuba lives outside Khabarovsk and works with alcoholics, using hypnosis and bioenergetics.[4] She told about the mag-nificent taiga around the village of Krasnyi Yar, the moun-tains and waterfalls, and the excitement of hunting for gin-seng. Ginseng is not easy to find, she said – its spirit reveals itself only to certain people at certain times. If you find some you must shout loudly, so that the spirits know that you appreciate their gift.

Lyuba said that all the grandmothers of Krasnyi Yar went out and picketed the government buildings in Vladivostok with Greenpeace to stop the logging. The logging company office is now locked up and deserted – for how long, nobody knows.

Lyuba went through a period where she thought she

needed new glasses, and then realized she was seeing auras, energy patterns and colours around people's bodies. She became very ill for several months and then enrolled in a course on bioenergetics or energy healing. She learned refined techniques that are proving very effective in her work with alcoholics and other sick people. And she herself is perfectly healthy. Perhaps this is how the spirits are choosing their workers these days. When I saw her during a quick visit in 1997, Lyuba told me that she had learned that she has shamanic ancestry. She promised to try to keep the loggers out of Krasnyi Yar until I come back. I want to know if the spirits will let me find ginseng!

6

Gvasyugi Storytelling

Two years later, in August 1995, I came back to the Khabarovsk Territory. Again Nadia Kimonko met me, this time as an old friend. We went straight to Gvasyugi.

Some things had changed, some were the same. The electricity was still on only part-time, people were working in their gardens. Valentina was even busier than before, still working as head of the village administration and finding building materials at a nearby Russian village, now nearly deserted because the logging was finished in the area and work had dried up.[1] She was planning to build a cultural centre and open-air museum. I frequently saw her solving arguments in the street.

The same kind of floating log bridge still crossed the river, but it was new. The old one had washed away in a flood in 1994. Valentina described going around the village streets in boats. Such floods happen regularly every ten to

Valentina Tunsyanovna Kyalundzyuga and Nadezhda Efimovna
Kimonko, standing in front of the village library, Gvasyugi.

fifteen years, so no one was surprised.

There was a new Mexican soap opera, "Wild Rose." The
heroine wore a baseball cap. She never acquired the obses-
sive popularity of the more traditionally feminine Maria,
who was now making commercials.

A woman who walked to Gvasyugi every day from a village
seven kilometres away to work at the weather station had

recently seen a tiger on her way. This was a shock, as people usually don't see tigers. It meant either that the tiger was ill or that his habitat had shrunk radically.[2] She ran, but the tiger did not chase her. The weather station itself was interesting – both rainfall and wind speed were measured by mechanical means, without electric devices, and a sign told how to judge visibility by looking at the mountains: "If you can see the first range, visibility is so many metres, the second, so many more, and the third ..."

Hyundai seemed to have stopped work in Krasnyi Yar, at least for the time being. American ecologists were visiting Gvasyugi, proposing the development of cottage industry. They were greeted cautiously, since they had no direct connections in the village. The needs of post-Soviet society require dealing with both the development of self-reliance and the habit of expecting aid to come from the central government. As always, the key to success lies in personal connections.

Tosia was away fishing and we moved into the "hotel," a single room with a leaky roof behind the library. There were two beds and an electric kettle. We boiled water at night and kept it in a thermos for morning tea when the electricity was off.

Both Anna Dinchuevna and Grandpa Kostya had died. Nanai shaman Mingo Geiker had said that Anna should have been a shaman herself – that was what her constant headaches indicated. Doctors had diagnosed a brain tumour. Anna was a staunch Communist party worker, so she had refused the shamanic gift all her life. According to Mingo and many local people, this made her constant illness and early death inevitable. At the same time the western medical system had let her down because of its inadequate facilities.

But there was a shaman in Gvasyugi this time, visiting her daughter. Adikhini told us she was over ninety years of age (although Nadia doubted it) and sometimes it was hard for her to call her spirits. But Valentina wanted to take Adikhini by boat out to a spit somewhere up the river for a picnic. We would take her drum and see what happened.

Adikhini was a tiny woman in high-top sneakers, her glasses held on by elastic. She claimed to be terrified of riding in the boat. We arrived at a good spot and got the fire going. Valentina instructed her granddaughter Marina not to stir the fire "or Grandfather *Podya* will be angry!" The spirit of fire is sometimes seen as male and sometimes female. Fire is believed to have a cleansing property and also unifies a clan. Metal is inimical to fire, which is why Marina was not to stir it with a metal object. It is also forbidden to put garbage into a fire that has been started for sacred purposes.

Adikhini made us all put on the *yampa* one by one and take up the drum. The drum's oval frame is made of lightweight, flexible bird-cherry wood, hollowed out so the sound of the stick on the frame resonates. Its head is made of goat-skin. Shaman's drums vary in size – Adikhini's was about 18" x 24" while some are much larger. They are often very shallow, only two or three inches deep. There are sounding pieces of metal attached to the inside of the rim and loose crossed leather thongs for a handle. The player holds the drum by the thongs with the head down and strikes it from underneath. At the same time the drum is moved up and down, thus producing three sounds – the stick striking the head, the hand holding the crossed thongs striking the head from inside (poosible because the drum is so shallow), and the metal pieces ringing. The belt is shaped in the form of a snake and has cone-shaped bells in the back that ring with the dancing. Valentina's husband went first – he was a very good dancer and drummer and had performed the role of the shaman for many years in dance ensembles. Adikhini was pleased. Valentina took her turn and then Nadia, both of whom played the drum and swayed their hips to make the bells on the belt sound.

Then it was my turn. It was only afterward that they told me you are *supposed* to make the shaman laugh – the laugh-

Udegei shaman Adikhini holding her shaman's drum at a picnic on the river Khor.

ter is part of raising the energy for the ceremony (called *samasini* in Udegei.) I was glad to hear it since it was not easy to coordinate the necessary movements of the hips with the rhythm of the drum. My admiration grew for this elderly woman who danced so gracefully although she walked with a cane.

The part of the ceremony where everyone present plays the drum is called *gongui*. Later just the assistants play – this is called *jagditi*. Drumming by all participants is the first step in calling the shaman's spirits. As the assistants play the spirits come closer, and when at last the shaman starts to drum, the spirits come very close and may even enter the shaman.

In spite of our efforts, Adikhini did not raise her spirits that day. Valentina told me that Adikhini still conducted shamanic ceremonies and also made divinations using a stone. She visualized the stone as being in front of her and read answers to questions based on its movements. This apparently worked much the same way as the pendulums I later saw used for divination in Bulava.

When we got back to Gvasyugi, Valentina told me about other shamans who used to work in Gvasyugi. One man, Kufesa Kimonko, was known for having someone shoot him in the chest with an arrow, which sent him into an altered state of consciousness called *otkini*. Afterward he had no scar from the arrow.

Grandmother Gounya was the last really strong Udegei shaman. She died in 1965. She not only healed people but also accompanied souls to *Buni*, the next world. In Udegei, that ritual is called *khanyaunya khuni* (like the Nanai *Kasa*). *Khanya* means soul. It was Gounya who accompanied the soul of Jansi Kimonko, the first Udegei writer, when he died in 1949.

Kimonko had hunted a bear in the wrong season and therefore the bear had killed him. In the struggle he had wounded the bear seriously. His relatives felt that because he had died what was "not his own death," meaning that he had died by violence, his soul needed to be accompanied – he would not find his way alone. They went far up the Gvasyuginka river for the ceremony. Through the shaman Kimonko's spirit spoke some final words to those present and then people gave him gifts of food and even money for the long road ahead. Then Gounya took his soul, which she had transferred into a hay figure, and went on a long visionary journey, entering a distant mountain that led to the land of the dead. It was dark there. When they arrived, she passed his soul on to deceased members of his family, whose identity was confirmed by people present at the ceremony. Then she returned to this world, with the help of her assistants who pulled on a leather strap which they had previously tied around her waist.[3] Before he died Kimonko told Valentina that she would be the support of her people, a prediction that has certainly been realized.

Valentina's great-uncle died when she was thirty-six and the mother of four. Valentina was disturbed at the way the ceremony was carried out and got sick. Gounya determined that the uncle had taken her soul with him and made Valentina a special dress and amulet to wear. She then scolded his spirit and he gave Valentina's soul up, saying he hadn't noticed he was taking her along. "I just tucked her under my arm!" he said.

Valentina also described one of Gounya's healings.

GOUNYA

If a small child was sick, Gounya would divine using her drum, addressing her spirits. She asks if there is a soul in the child. If the soul is gone and the child is three or under, *Sagdi-mama* will have taken him. She is the one who keeps the souls of children in her nest before their birth. These souls are in the form of the little birds we see embroidered on the wedding dress. If there will be many children, there are many souls in the nest. When the child is sick, she has taken him back. So the shaman asks if the soul is with *Sagdi-mama*. If it is, she says, "I need to shamanize to bring the soul back."

People prepare a pole with three branches. A nest is made in the top from dry hay and *khatka*, the kind of soft swamp grass that is used in shoes to keep the feet warm and comfortable. Then they sew a special round amulet of skin in the form of a foetus – like a crescent moon that almost meets. The sick child wears this amulet. The shaman will breathe the child's soul into the amulet. All these things must be prepared before the ceremony begins.

The ledum plant is burned and Gounya calls the spirits, walking around the house with special movements, gathering everything that will be needed. She tells where she is going. She turns into a bird, a cuckoo, and sits on a tree. She turns into a butterfly and flies. *Sagdi-mama* must not notice that she is approaching or what she is up to. The shaman admires the nest, saying, "Oh, you have so many children!" Quickly she grabs the soul and puts it in her mouth to bring it back safely. Meanwhile the sick child and mother are sitting next to the shaman.

Sagdi-mama sees everything about the child and speaks to the mother through the shaman, saying, for example, "I see a bruise," naming its exact location. It may be something that happened long ago and is healed now. *Sagdi-mama* asks how it happened, and the mother tells her. *Sagdi-mama* says, "If this child is not better cared for I will take him back altogether."

The mother promises, and the shaman returns to this world, dancing away from the people. Now the mother must sing a special song, "*dokhonye*," meaning, "Come to me my child, I'll make you toys." Things like that. Now the shaman breathes the soul onto the amulet and places it on the drum. It jumps around as she plays and finally jumps into the hem of the mother's dress. She catches it, and from there they put it in the nest on the pole. After that the soul returns to the body, and after about a month they get rid of that pole, either burning it or taking it away. ▼

In 1999 I met Gounya's granddaughter Onya, who now teaches the Udegei language at the Gvasyugi school. She recalls living with Gounya, saying that they were very poor but sometimes food would appear on their doorstep, a gift from people who wanted a ceremony done. Later in the evening the people would arrive and Gounya would carefully cover all the windows and do what was needed. Onya says her grandmother made special figures for people depending on what they needed. For example, one woman had chronic diarrhea and Gounya made a hollow doll, plugged at the bottom. The woman fed the doll food through the mouth and only pulled the plug occasionally when the doll was full.

Nadia and I paid a visit to Dusia, who divined answers to our questions using forked sticks. Two people sat opposite each other, holding the sticks so that they connected in the middle. The ends had been dipped in water. The sticks moved up and down, together and apart, in answer to questions, and the diviner interpreted the movements. I learned what kind of amulet I should make to help my mother's heart. Nadia was told to make a certain kind of paper hat to help a headache.

Some say the climate here used to be much warmer. Nadia remembers that her grandmother used to tell stories about monkeys and crocodiles, which she didn't believe. Valentina said there is a swamp far away up the river Khor where the water is red, from mineral deposits. That reminded me of tales of healing water, like "Yegdyga and the Seal." She told me, "people say there used to be crocodiles in that swamp, who chased people and ate them. People killed the crocodiles by burning birch-bark and throwing it in the water. The crocodiles took the flaming birch-bark in their mouths and died. Beside the Sukpai river there is a lake where people find cowrie shells. They send a dog into the water, the shells stick to the dog and then the dog comes back and they take the shells off and use them to decorate clothing. Once in every hundred years this lake floods and many people are killed."[4]

Valentina also told a story about monkeys, another animal that could not survive today's climate in the Amur region.

THE MONKEYS

Kanda Mafa lived with his children, two girls and one older brother. Once the older sister said to the younger, "Let's fly to heaven."

"Go by yourself," said the younger, "I don't want to."

So the older sister took the shaman's drum. She started to sing and then said, "Brother, when you go hunting in the taiga tomorrow, you're going to meet two people. Check out their breasts, and then marry them."

The next day, he woke up and set out to go hunting. He walked and walked and came to a hill, a mountain. There were big rocks. He looked up, and then went on. Suddenly he saw two people sitting there. He approached and at that time the ties on his skis broke.

He came up to those people and felt their breasts and they were women. And they took him along with them.

At home time went by. A day passed and another, and still he was gone. Many days went by. And then the younger sister said, "Sister, you made this happen. Now you bring him back. Those two monkeys in the mountain came and took him away and now they are keeping him in the mountains, sucking his blood. He's become just skin and bones."

"All right," said the older sister, and the two of them started to drum and sing their shaman's songs. The older sister flew but she didn't have enough strength and couldn't bring him back.

"Younger sister," she said, "I can't bring him back. You try, namude, namusa."

"You called those bad spirits, but now you can't bring him back. Our brother is dying. We've got to save him."

"I can't do it. I don't have enough strength. You try."

So the younger sister sang and drummed, flying to her spirits, but she couldn't get there. She tried a second time and still didn't have the strength. The third time she gathered all her strength and flew to those rocks. She took her brother and dragged him out of there. He flew, looking thin as a shirt. They got him back and healed him. And that's how the younger sister brought her brother back from those monkeys.

They lived.

Again one evening the older sister started to sing. She took the drum and sang shamanic songs. Then she said to the younger sister, "Two men are coming our way. Let's marry them."

The younger sister said, "Again you are going to call trouble on our house." The older one finished drumming and a little later two Yegdyga, two men, arrived. One sat down on the older sister's side and the other on the younger sister's. The younger sister immediately lay down, covered herself up, and didn't get up. But the older went here and there doing everything. She gave the man food, looking after him.

Then he went away and she said, "I'm going too, I'm going to marry him."

They went away. But the younger sister refused to get married, she wouldn't go with those monkeys.

And so those monkeys took away her sister and she died. When people went and looked for her they found she had died. The younger sister said, "What she was looking for, she found. It was impossible to save her."

So that's it about the monkeys. They lived in the rocks

and when they rolled back and forth, they called, "Tsyoo, tsyoo, papandasyoo!" ▼

Here again we see a kind of divination through shamanic singing and drumming. In this story the monkeys have transformed into evil spirits.

Valentina told some of the same stories as the last time I had been there, with slight variations. One difference was that this time I told Valentina I wanted to write about shamans, so she pointed them out in various stories where the shaman had not been named the first time – like the girl sending her brother off with the comb and the sharpening stone in "Yegdyga and the Bones." She had used singing and drumming to learn what to do.

The monkey story was new, and so was this next one, although it repeats familiar themes. It also showed Valentina's talents as a comic, pouting, boasting, threatening with the hunting bag!

PALAM PADU[5] – THE HUNTER'S BAG

Palam Padu hung there on the wall for a long time, probably people forgot about it. The bag got sick of hanging there and one day he took off! Well after all, it's a story!

He took off down the river. Along came a bear. "Palam Padu, where are you going?"

"I'm looking for something to eat. I think I'll eat you."

"How can you eat me? You're just a small bag!"

"I will!" And the bag took the bear and swallowed him.

On he went. Next he met a tiger. "Where are you going, Palam Padu?"

"I'm looking for food. I think I'll eat you."

"How could you, a little hunter's bag, eat me, a big tiger?"

"I *will* eat you!" And Palam Padu took the tiger and

Udegei shaman's belt – *yampa* – worn by Dmitrii Kyalundzyuga.

swallowed him. He swallowed him whole and then walked and walked and came out on the shore of the sea.

People were living on the other side. How could he get across? He didn't need any boat. He just drank the sea up! Everything, the fish and all. That's what Palam Padu was like. He went across and arrived on the other side.

He saw that Kanda Mafa was living there with his wife and daughter. "Kanda Mafa," he said, "Give me your daughter to marry."

"You mouldy old bag, where have you been lying around? And now you want to marry my daughter! Who needs you?"

"So you don't want to agree? All right, I'm going to let my bear go on you."

"A bear?!"

"I will. Let your daughter marry me." And again Kanda Mafa complained. "You bag, where haven't you been? And now you want to marry my daughter."

"So you don't want to? I'll let this bear go."

And he opened his mouth and out came the bear with a roar. And he started chasing the old man and the old woman. And the old man couldn't run, he was crawling.

"Stop, stop," he cried. "Call off your bear and I'll let you marry my daughter." The old man was out of breath.

Palam Padu called off the bear.

The old man rested, then he said, "After all, you're just a bag, not a person. And you keep asking for my daughter. I didn't bring her up to marry a hunting bag, Palam Padu."

"Are you going to give her to me or not?"

"No, I won't."

"All right, I'm going to send my tiger after you." So he opened his mouth and out flew the tiger. And he started to chase the old man who ran and ran and ran and ran. He couldn't run any more and fell down and crawled! He called out, "Call off your tiger. I'll let you marry my daughter."

The bag took the tiger back. The man caught his breath, came to his senses and started to think. "I will not give you my daughter. I need to find a man for her, who will feed us when we get old, who will be rich so that later there will be plenty. A bag is just a bag. What will you give me? Nothing. No I won't give her to you. I did not bring this girl up just to give her away to a simple hunting bag."

"So, you don't want to? You're deceiving me? All right I'm going to let the water go so that there will be a terrible flood and all your things will wash away." And he opened up and let the water out. It flowed here and it flowed there. The old woman and everybody climbed up a tree. They sat there one day, two days – they got hungry. The bag just stayed there waiting to see what the old man would say.

"Enough, Palam Padu," he said at last. "You will marry my daughter. Just take this water away. We're hungry."

"You won't trick me?"

"No, no, I won't trick you. Just take this water away."

So Palam Padu swallowed the water and took that Belye away, their daughter. They went away to his own land and the old people stayed where they were. And the bag hung himself back up on the pole.

Belye lived and lived there. She went hunting and did everything for herself. One night she got mad and took that bag down and threw it aside.

"Am I really going to live my whole life alone? I could have married somebody and now I have nobody, just this bag hanging there."

She was mad. She just threw it away somewhere, and then lay down to sleep. She slept and slept and when she woke up it was light. She thought, "What's happened, have I overslept? Maybe I got mad and overslept."

She got up and went outside and there the stars were still shining. "What's going on?" She went back in and there was Yegdyga, so beautiful, lying next to that Palam Padu. Light was shining from the beautiful young man.

And it turned out that Palam Padu had turned into a handsome man. And so she took that Palam Padu and hid it. And they were married! ▼

Elements combine and recombine – the girl with a mysterious husband (what could be a better provider than a hunting bag?), her waking to light in the house. Palam Padu swallowed animals the way a shaman acquires helpers, and they later helped him.

The next tale Valentina told explains the appearance of one constellation, the Pleiades. I later heard a similar Nanai tale, both of which involve frogs who are bad housekeepers and the testing of a new bride.[6]

SIX BROTHERS AND THE SQUIRRELS[7]

Six brothers lived together with their sister Belye. The six went hunting and the sister cooked for them. She sewed *uli* and clothes.

Once the brothers arrived home and said that along the way they had seen an army of squirrels coming their way. The brothers hid their sister in the ashes of the hearth. They put blood on top. Then they fed fat to the skin beater, the door, and the smoke-hole. They forgot only a piece of an old boot. These were simple boots not for hunting but just for going outdoors. Then the brothers flew away to heaven.

The squirrels came and started to ask, "Smoke-hole, where are your masters?"

"They fed me fat. I won't tell anybody!"

"Door, where are your masters?"

"They fed me. I won't tell."

The piece of old boot came along and said, "They didn't feed me any fat. I'll tell! The six brothers flew to heaven and they buried their younger sister in the ashes."

The squirrels beat the smoke-hole and poked the ashes with a spear. One squirrel got blood on his spear. They were sure they had killed Belye, and went away. Belye came out, got the fire going and burned the piece of old boot. She got ready to leave, loaded up the enclosed *aiolu* (half sled), hitched up the dog, and tied a willow broom on behind. "Broom, brush away our tracks so that they won't find us," she said.

The dog ran, and the brush swept the snow. Then the sled got stuck on a hummock in the swamp. From the hump came Emenda with messy hair and her eyes sticking out. "Who ran into my house? Ka ka ka," she said, sounding like a frog.

Belye went into the house and saw two old frogs and some little ones beside them. "Emenda, what are these frogs?"

"They are my parents."

"I can't live with them," says Belye. She took the frogs on the hem of her dress and threw them onto another hummock. Belye started to live with Emenda. Belye went hunting. She brought in a reed and put it beside the bed. She washed her hair, took off her embroidered robe. Then the dog began to bark.

"Emenda, go and look."

"There's nobody there. The leaves are just rustling from the wind." Again the dog barked. Suddenly they heard two men's voices talking outside. Belye didn't even have time to dress before they came in. She turned into the reed. The older brother sat on Emenda's side and the younger on the other. Next day they got ready to go. Emenda put on Belye's embroidered dress and took off her own of fishskin.

When they were on the way, the younger brother said he had forgotten his small knife. Emenda said, "Why go back? You'll make a new one." But the younger brother didn't listen and went back.

He came in and heard a voice saying, "Emenda took my

dress and left her dirty one." Yegdyga came in unexpected-
ly. Belye tried to turn into that plant again but she stayed
half plant and half person.

Yegdyga said, "How will you live alone? Come with me."
The two caught up with the older brother.

Kanda Mafa and his wife were waiting – they kept going
out and looking at the road. At last the old woman saw
them and said, "Our children are coming. There are four
of them. Lay silk from the threshold, make up the beds.
We will greet our daughters-in-law." Emenda came first
along the silk and sat down on the bed. Belye came, took
up the silk, turned back the bedding and sat. The old people were pleased to see such a tidy woman. And so they
lived.

Then Kanda Mafa said to Emenda, "My bones are old. I
want to warm them by the fire. Get a good fire going."

Emenda ran to the woods and brought lilac wood. She
got a big fire going and said, "Sit close." Old Kanda Mafa
sat close to the fire. Flames shot up, sparks flew in all
directions. The old man shouted, "Why did you use lilac
wood?" and he ran away. "Old woman, put this fire out or
we will burn up."

And so they went on living.

Then Kanda Mafa said, "Bride of my elder son, in my
old age I want kasha made of grain." Emenda ran outside,
took a pot and ran to the shore. She took sand and put it
on to boil. When it boiled, she took it off and said to the
old man, "Come and eat. Put your spoon in deep!" Kanda
Mafa took a big wooden spoon, reached in deep, took kasha
and put it in his mouth and began to shout, "What kind of
kasha is this, made of sand? Old woman, throw it out!"

And so they lived. Then Kanda Mafa says, "Bride of my
older son, I'm old and will soon die. I want to look at your
parents and brothers."

"I can invite them," said Emenda, and ran out.

Kanda Mafa said, "Old woman, make the beds with silk.
We will greet our guests."

Emenda came running. She brought frogs on the hem of her dress. Big and small, she dumped them out on the bed. They jumped around, making garunking sounds. "Old woman, take them away!" shouted Kanda Mafa.

And so they lived.

And then Kanda Mafa turned to the wife of his younger son. "Bride of my younger son, get the fire going. My bones are old and I want to get warm."

"Can I fulfil your request? I don't know what kind of wood to prepare."

"Too bad," he said, "but you must."

She went out and came to a dry tree. She sat down there and fell asleep. She woke up and the firewood was ready. She picked it up and went back. She got the fire going and invited the old man. "Come warm your bones," she said. "But sit a little further away so you don't get burnt."

Kanda Mafa warmed his bones and was content. And so they lived.

And then one day Kanda Mafa said, "Bride of my younger son, cook some kasha for me in my old age."

"Where will I find it?" She went out and along a path into the woods. She came to the dry tree and fell asleep. When she woke up she saw a bag. She took it, went back, cooked the kasha and said, "Eat carefully. Don't burn yourself. Take a little from the top." Kanda Mafa took the wooden spoon and ate carefully. The kasha was tasty and the old man was happy.

Then he said, "Bride of my younger son, invite your brothers and sisters. I want to see them before I die."

"*Ado*, where will I find them? I had brothers at one time. I would like to fulfil your request but I don't know where they are."

"Too bad. But invite them." Old man Kanda Mafa insisted. Belye went out along the path. She came to the dry tree and unnoticed fell asleep. She woke up and saw her seven brothers. They said, "You woke up. Now let's go to

Kanda Mafa." Kanda Mafa heard their voices and said, "Lay silk from the threshold to the bed. Guests are coming."

They made a big holiday. As they were leaving the brothers said, "We will not come to you any more. You live here with your husband and we will marry seven girls, the *Vagda*" (the Pleiades). ▼

The next tale begins like a Nanai tale told by Maria Beldi[8] but it takes a different turn when the first wife takes her revenge on the toad and proves her own worth. At the same time the tale explains why toads live under rocks.

TOAD WIFE

Kanda Mafa and his wife had a daughter. She was little, sitting in a cradle. He caught fish with a fish trap called *kha*, made of willow. One morning he came to look and saw – no fish but instead *utya* – a toad.

He said, "You've driven away all my fish. I'm going to throw you out."

The toad spoke in a human voice and said, "Don't throw me out, old man."

"Who will you be to me, a daughter or sister? Or do you want to be my wife?"

"Yes," said the toad, "I want to be your wife." So the old man took her home in the bottom of his coat – he didn't say anything about it to his wife. He laid the toad in his box, *atoya*, and covered her up.

When they ate the old man asked for the tastiest pieces. His wife was surprised. "Better give the best parts to the child," she said. He shouted at her and ate turned to the wall. The old woman was surprised and when he went away she started to look through his bedding. She found the *atoya*, opened the cover, and saw the toad.

"Why is the old man keeping you? As a sister, a daughter, or as a second wife?"

"Yes, he is keeping me as a second wife," said the toad. The old woman was angry. She took *utya* out and began to beat her with a stick. But it didn't even hurt the toad. Then the old woman threw her in the creek but she crawled out of the water. She threw her in the fire but she jumped out unharmed. The old woman beat her again - then put her back in the case and closed the cover.

The old man came back from fishing and began to ask for the tastiest pieces. He turned to the wall and whispered. The toad didn't eat anything. When the old woman went out the old man began to ask, "Why don't you eat?"

"Your wife beat me. She put me in the water and the fire!" The old man was angry. He ran out, took a stick and began to beat his wife.

She was angry and got ready to go away. She said to the toad, "If you want to dry your husband's boots, hang them on his ear. If you want to feed the dog, then pour the hot stuff right into his mouth." So she spoke and went out of the house.

The old man stayed in the house with the little girl and his second wife.

The old man took off his boots. The toad took them and tried to hang them on his ear.

"What are you doing?" he said. The old man was angry and went out. The dogs were hungry. She started to pour hot food right in their mouths. The dogs started to run away. The old man caught them. The hungry little girl started to cry and couldn't be calmed. The old man was even angrier.

He picked the child up, put the toad outside, took a stick and started to beat her. But it didn't hurt. He put her in the water and she came out – he put her in the fire and she jumped out. The old man took the child and went looking for his first wife. He was walking along and suddenly that toad jumped right on his back. He was angry.

"I want to be your wife," she called.

"I don't need that kind of wife!" He grabbed the toad and put a big rock on top of her. Then he found his first wife and they began to live together again. And from that time on toads have hidden under rocks. ▼

The next story continues with the fate of many sisters and evil spirits. It is the only mention I have heard of cannibalism in this area. This terrifying story also explains the creation of swamp formations, linking it to mythic tales of creation.

SEVEN GIRLS

There lived seven girls. The oldest provided for the younger ones. She went hunting and collected berries. But for some reason there got to be fewer and fewer animals in the taiga and she had to go further and further. She was hungry.

She met an old woman and ate her. She liked it. She started coming back to her sisters after one day or two bringing no food. Even seven days she would be gone. She didn't talk or laugh with her sisters any more. She turned away from them all and lay down to sleep.

One evening the younger sisters decided to make their elder sister laugh. They did everything – they jumped over the fire, danced, and laughed. Still the elder sister didn't laugh, didn't talk. The younger sisters threw out streamers of bird-cherry wood, they pushed each other, jumped through the fire – it was such fun!

When the elder sister opened her mouth her teeth showed and the younger ones saw a scary thing. The elder sister had teeth that were black from human hair. They realized that from hunger she had become a cannibal.

The next day the younger sisters decided to make them-

selves skis and run away from the older one. They made
them any way they could. Instead of tying hers with rope,
the youngest used a chain.

In the evening the older sister came home and lay
down. She went away in the morning. As soon as she was
gone the younger ones put on their skis and began to run
away. The youngest went first and the second sister came
last. They saw the oldest one coming after them saying,
"*nakusaa* – straps on the skis, break!"

The straps broke for that second sister.

The older sister ate her up. While she was eating the
others ran away.

The older one came after them calling, "Straps, break!
Chygda, puchky." All the younger sisters' straps broke and
the older sister ate them all. Her belly began to grow. She
could hardly move.

Only the youngest was left. She came out on the shore
and saw that on the other side sat Yegdyga.

She called to him, "Yegdyga, bring me over. Our older
sister is chasing me and she has eaten all my sisters."
Yegdyga brought her over and hid her in the barn. He
had just hidden her when out on the shore came the
older sister – big belly, hair loose and messy.

She shouted, "Yegdyga, bring me over. I fell behind my
sisters."

"Go up stream, there's a boat there," he answered. "You
can get across."

She ran there to the crossing and called, "There's nothing there!"

Then he said, "Go downstream. There's a boat there."
She ran there with her messy hair streaming behind. Then
she ran back.

"There's nothing there."

"I forgot. The boat is here. I'll bring you across." He
went to bring her over and in the middle of the river he
rocked the boat. The elder sister fell in the water and the
current carried her away. That big belly got in her way; she

couldn't get out of the water.

She called out, "May humps grow in the swamp from my head. From my bones, impassable bushes. And from my guts twining plants." She drowned.

After that the hummocks were formed, and the bushes so thick that it's hard for hunters to walk through the forest.

But the younger sister married Yegdyga! ▼

Valentina went on to tell one more tale from her battered notebook of transcriptions, a story told by the elder Ekhunda in the 1960s. Like the tales of marriage with bears and tigers, this story shows another situation where the usual marriage pattern does not work – here the parents refuse to give their daughter up. It is possible that the seven brothers in the story were destined to marry her. The girl reverts to the more ancient way and marries a man whom she has raised as a younger brother.9

BELYE AND NAUNDYAKA

A man and his wife lived by the shore of the sea with their daughter, Belye. She grew up and became beautiful. She was a master of all hands – she could embroider beautiful designs and sewed robes for the old man and woman. She sewed herself a wedding dress.

Her father thought and then said, "Daughter, I will not give you up. You are our only child. When we are old, who will look after us?"

"Then build me a house out over the sea so nobody can come to me." So she spoke to the old people.

The old man built the house out over the sea for his daughter and she lived there. The wind blew, the house rocked. Once a strong hurricane came up. The house couldn't hold up and it fell into the sea. In the house was Belye.

The house rode the sea. Once it passed seven brothers, Yegdygas. Belye asked for their help.

"Seven brothers, catch my house. I will sew clothes for you. I will cook food for you."

The brothers answered, "We have a bride. We are getting ready to go there. She lives with old man Kanda Mafa and his old woman."

Belye went further in her house. Then at last it got caught on a sandy shore. Somehow she got out. Walking on the shore she saw a boy, Naundyaka. He was playing and caught fish with a harpoon and ate it immediately, without cooking it. She came closer and asked, "Naundyaka, whom do you live with?"

"I live alone. I have no one."

Belye stayed there to live with Naundyaka. She went hunting and shot from the bow and got a good take. She dressed in men's clothes when she went hunting. When she came home she put on a woman's dress. She dressed Naundyaka in new clothes and took care of him.

Once while Naundyaka was alone, seven brothers came and began asking, "Whom do you live with? Who sews for you?"

"I live with my brother," answered the boy.

"What brother? You have nobody." The seven brothers didn't believe him. They took his toy arrows and went away. Naundyaka was left alone and he cried.

In the evening Belye came home and saw his puffy eyes. "Who hurt you? Who was here?"

"There were seven brothers. They broke my bow."

Belye was angry. She put on her skis and set off fast, over the tops of the bushes. Snow flew behind her as if from a strong wind. She arrived at the seven brothers' place. She took the door-skin with her stick and threw it onto the shore.

She said, "Come out, seven brothers. We will compete in archery."

"Who has come to us? Who raises his voice to the seven

brothers?" They came out of their straw hut. Belye took off her earrings and hung them on a tree.

"If one of you can shoot through the hole in my earring – I will say you are a brave Yegdyga." They started with the oldest and nobody could hit the center. All the arrows flew past. Then just the youngest was left. The best shot.

"Show the braggart!" called the older brothers. The youngest let his arrow go but it too went past the earring.

Belye took the bow and let her arrow go. It went through the hole and flew out the other side. The seven brothers were defeated. She took her earrings down from the tree, put them on, and went home. She and Naundyaka got into a birchbark boat and sailed to an island. The seven brothers wanted to take revenge on Belye. The seven brothers got into a boat and rode to the island to take revenge for their disgrace. They came to the hut and nobody was there. On the island they saw a bear skin, which Belye had hung out.

Belye saw them and said, "Blow winds, more strongly." The wind came up strong, the sea got rough, the boat turned over, and the seven brothers drowned. The wind and sea calmed down. Belye and the boy Naundyaka went back to their birchbark hut and began to live peacefully. She probably married him. She brought up a husband for herself. ▼

What follows is another version of the "Ice Mountain" which Valentina told in 1993. This time she emphasizes the heroine's practicality, perhaps in response to an article I had written about the protective power of embroidered designs. She praised my article and then retold the story – which seemed to be her way of teaching me not to get too metaphoric in my interpretations. Doye himself now admires Gamuli's bravery and strength. He even apologizes to her for trying to kill her.

Later I saw a copy of Valentina's transcription of the story as it was told by an elder thirty years ago.[10] In that version

Valentina Tunsyanovna Kyalundzyuga and her granddaughter
Marina. Winter 1999.

Gamuli "thought" of Doye before setting out – Valentina
says she may have seen him in a vision. There was no ethno-
graphic description of articles in the home, although it was
mentioned that the traditional house had both male and
female sides. In that version the drama is drawn out by
Gamuli catching the knife and throwing it back at Doye
before he finally wounds her. The heroine also says that she

steps across the arrow on purpose, to pay Doye back because he tried to kill her, the implication being that her magic in breaking that taboo would be strong enough to kill him. Comparing these tales provides good examples of the way traditional tellers change details to get various points across and of how tales change from one generation to the next.

GAMULI

Yegdyga lives on an ice cliff or mountain. He is considered strong – if he says so, the wind blows. He lives on that ice mountain. So, our Belye – she was such an artist – began to sew a robe for herself, all covered with designs. Then she decided to try the ice mountain. She knew that if anybody could make it up there she would marry him. This would be good for her. Everyone knew it.

Everyone knew that she was strong and that he would choose a bride only from among girls like her. She was an artist and a strong woman. She decided to test her strength and find a husband for herself.

She got ready to go, put on her robe – it was so beautiful. She had also sewed leggings and boots with embroidered designs, and on top she put a coat of fishskin. It wouldn't let the wind through. And on top of her beautiful boots she put boots of fishskin.

She got dressed, put on her skis and set off. Toward evening she came to another girl who asked her, "What news have you brought me?"

"There is an ice mountain, and on the ice mountain is a hut where Yegdyga lives with his mother. If a girl can make it up there, he will take her as his wife."

"Let me go with you."

"Let's go then." And the second girl got dressed but her dress was poorer, with fewer designs. She didn't put on a fishskin coat. They went the next day at dawn.

They came to a third Belye. In the evening they told her everything and she decided to come too. Her dress was a patchwork of strips and pieces of cloth, with no embroidery. This was a sure sign of poverty.[11] She got dressed up as well as she could and the three continued on their way.

And around noon they got to the ice mountain. When the sun shone on the ice, it reflected so brightly that it hurt to look. They bent down so the sun wouldn't be in their eyes and kept going. Our Belye had a stick – on one end a little shovel and on the other end a sharp hook. She hooked on and climbed.

The mother sang "Doye, Doye! Three girls are coming up to you. Choose the best artist. Test their strength – let the winds go!"

Doye called "Wind, wind, rise, fill out." And the wind came up. It got dark as dark.

The last girl, who was poorly dressed, slipped and fell down.

Two girls were left.

The sun came out and they began to go up together.

Then the mother said, "Two girls are left. Raise the wind – test them!" Again the wind came up – a big storm. It was dark. They kept coming up. Our Belye had her fish-skin coat, so it didn't blow through. She kept coming up and the other one got cold but she too kept coming. The wind got stronger and the second Belye slipped down the ice mountain.

Again the wind went down, the sun came out. Only Belye Gamuli was left. She hooked on and made steps, and came up and up. From up top the mother sang, "Only one is left. She is not dressed beautifully. She is no artist. Blow hard so that she will fall. What do you want with that kind of bride?"

"But she is brave," he said, "she keeps coming higher." Again the wind came up stronger, whistling. It grew so dark. Our Belye kept coming up. The wind was blowing. At last she came out on top, grabbed the door of their house with her stick and threw it away. The wind took it and carried it to the sea.

He was angry. "Who dares to do this?"

She entered and sat down. From where he lay, he took up a knife, threw it, and wounded her leg. She cut off a piece of her embroidery and put it under his bedding. Then she got up angrily and went on her way, wounded. She started to go down the mountain, angry with him.

"She's no artist," he said, "and she wanted to marry me! Now she's angry and gone away."

Then the mother found the embroidery and said, "She is an artist. Look what beautiful designs she made! Go catch up with her." He was ashamed. It turned out she was such an artist and had just put on the fishskin so the wind wouldn't blow through her.

She was on her way down. He took his spear and threw it. This was the spear he used for hunting bear and wild boar. He threw it so it fell across her path. She was just about to step over. But because it was sacred and a woman was forbidden to step over it, she hesitated. It is considered *sondo*, a sin.

He called, "Don't step over." Then he started to apologize. "I didn't realize you were an artist. You are strong and have beaten all the rest. I want to marry you. I'll heal your wound. Just don't step over my spear!"

Well, her goal was to get married so she stopped. He caught up and healed her. With his first finger he took saliva and went three times around the wound, and it got well. And that's how she won and they got married! ▾

I asked if stepping across the spear would take away his strength. Valentina agreed and said that it shows a lack of respect to the hunter and is in general shameful. Next I asked if Belye's marriage to the Master of the Wind showed that she had gotten connected with a spirit, as if it were her shamanic initiation. Valentina said it was not, but pointed out that he was a healer, using his finger to heal the wound. "He was also clairvoyant (as was his mother), seeing who was coming up the mountain. And Gamuli defeated him. He wanted to see only what was on the surface. But she dressed practically, because in the wind that skin coat doesn't blow through. To live in the taiga you must know what to wear. Those other girls just wore simple materials, and they were the losers."

Valentina and many other indigenous storytellers believe that it is dangerous to speak directly of the inner lives of shamans. But the stories may be a way to speak of that reality obliquely, just as deities like the bear and tiger are called by nicknames. Subtle ways of "speaking around" the subject protect the speaker. To call these multi-layered stories shamanic in a narrow sense is an oversimplification, although they do reflect shamanic philosophy.

7

Ul'chi Storytelling
in Bulava

On my first visit Nadia had talked about the Ul'chi people, another Tungus-language people who live further down the Amur. In the meantime I had met an Ul'chi specialist on shamanic culture, Nadezhda Duvan, who was with Mingo Geiker at the shamanism workshop I had attended in the United States. So I was eager to visit an Ul'chi village.

Nadia and I got up very early and walked through the rainy streets of Khabarovsk, down through the "Park of Culture and Rest," past rusting fairground rides and boarded up refreshment stands, to the riverboat station. Crowds were shoving to get onto the *Meteor*, the hydrofoil that goes down the Amur. Our destination was the village of Bulava. We had reserved tickets, so we shoved to the front of the line, got on, and found our seats. They were singularly uncomfortable and a long way from the dirty windows. My idea of a pleasant river cruise started to evaporate.

The Amur River at Bulava.

The trip to Bulava took fourteen hours with numerous stops at villages and at the city of Komsomolsk-na-Amure. Most of the outdoor parts of the boat were jammed with smokers, but there was a spot at the door where the breeze was fresh and I could watch the scenery pass by. The land is flat, often marshy. There are islands in the river and on some of them people like Leonid Maktuvich grow hay.

We ate our lunch of boiled eggs, cucumbers, bread and thermos tea and read newspapers. I was interested in the classified ads – sales of apartments and computers, men looking for women, women for men. But then my eye was struck by a headline: "Naikhin hospital closes – people turn to shamans." This is just what should be happening, in my opinion – a return to traditional medicine in the face of the breakdown of modern medical service. But it turned out the article merely deplored the closing of the hospital and the reference to shamans was not serious: it was a way of suggesting how primitive life had become.

At last the *Meteor* pulled in to the dock at Bulava. Many passengers got off and a crowd of friends and relatives met them. Three young people had been dispatched to meet us and took us to the home of Mado Dechuli and Kolya U. Bulava is long and spread out. It seemed to me, walking with heavy bags, that they must live at the very opposite end. But it turned out that "Old Bulava" was even further, up over the hill. The village has a beautiful location, surrounded by incredibly white birch trees with spectacular views of the river and faraway mountains.

I felt right at home with Mado and Kolya. Mado is a dancer and ensemble leader and Kolya is an artist, well known for his graphics and wood carving. Their two sons showed talent from both sides of the family. Their house was large, and wonderfully clean and simple in its furnishings. The place was a constant whirlwind of artistic activity.

In summer there is a cruise ship that comes down the Amur with tourists. When it stops at Bulava the children perform and artists sell craftwork. Supposedly the ship was coming the next day (although in fact it didn't). Costumes were being ironed, phone calls went back and forth with parents of dancing children, Mado tried to convince Kolya to put some of his work up for sale. Kolya didn't want to bother. This kind of activity reminded me of my own home. I felt accepted quickly and was allowed to make my own coffee. I didn't get to help with the dishes very often though. Hospitality is a strict tradition.

Mado made up a list of the storytelling grandmothers of Bulava and the next morning Nadia and I began visiting them. There were five Ul'chi shamans living at the time, four of them women. We would visit at least one of them too, said Mado.

First on the list was Ymynda Ycha, whose Russian name is Anna Pavlovna. She lived alone in a house in the same part of town as Mado. At first she didn't seem to remember any stories and told us about the house they used to live in before Soviet times.

"It was a big wooden house. Beside the door was the stove. Then the sleeping benches went all around inside the house. The stove and benches were made of stones. We'd get a big fire going, the stove would heat up, we'd set a pot right over the open fire, and cook like that. There were two openings in the benches, one on either end and the smoke went through before going out a hole in the wall.[1] It made the benches warm. Earth was sprinkled on the bench and then on top of that, a cover we made ourselves and then, the bedding, thin, not like these mattresses. But you could sleep on it and it didn't hurt. And now I can't sleep on three mattresses! So we all slept on benches around the house like that and a long pipe carried the smoke outside. The pipe was also made of stones, then spread with clay.

"We painted that kind of house with clay, and it became white. It was dark inside, under the roof. They painted the house once a year in the fall. The windows were not made of glass but of fishskin. You couldn't see through them but light came through. If you wanted to see, you took a needle and made a little hole. They were pretty and light in the fall when we made the new ones. Through the winter the smoke darkened the windows and by spring practically no light came through. Of course, since the stove was open, it smoked. There were also no electric lamps but they made lamps of fish oil and kept them in the corners. I don't know how people did all that carving and embroidery without light.

"Three or four families lived in one house. Mama, papa, my older sister, and I slept on this side. My younger brother slept in that corner, and my older brother slept in the other. Father's brother slept here too. Over on the other side lived a different family. It was warm. We wore shoes made of fishskin and filled with hay, soft swamp grass. Even in summer. Outer coats were made of fishskin and winter coats of dog fur. We also made boots of fur.

"We made threads of fishskin and also of some plant material and tendons. We took off the fishskin, dried it, then dampened, worked, and cut it. I also worked the threads, back when I had teeth; we made them very thin. Some of the skin we cut fine for designs. Then sew, sew, sew! But lately I haven't been taking off the fishskin."

She also described the way they kept the bear for the ritual. In the traditional bear ceremony, a family kept a young bear for one or two years and then sacrificed him. His soul was to return to the master of the taiga and report on the behaviour of humans on earth. The ceremony cleared the channels through which animals killed while hunting could take on new flesh and be reborn. It was accompanied by special music, dances, and foods. This kind of ceremony was carried out by the Ul'chi, Nivkh, and Ainu peoples, and not by the other peoples of the Amur. The fact that the Ul'chi, alone of the Tungus-speaking peoples, performed the ceremony can be explained by their close relationship with the Ainu, who used to live in the area around Bulava as well as on Sakhalin Island and intermarried with the Ul'chi.[2]

"The bear had a separate little house. There was a hole in the top and that was how we gave him food. His hut had

The bear's house, where the bear was kept in preparation for the
ceremony at Bulava in 1992.

hay on top – mama made it nice and warm. A couple of
years ago [in 1992] they had the ceremony here for the
first time since the late 1930s. They kept the bear for a couple of years in a hut that was open – how that bear suffered!
I couldn't even stand to look." I had heard that the suffering of the bear was the reason people had decided not to
do the ceremony again in the old way. From now on they
will do parts of the ritual and celebration but without keeping or killing a bear.[3]

Nadezhda described how the Ul'chi bear ceremony was
done.

UL'CHI BEAR CEREMONY

People would catch a bear cub and keep it for two to three years in a special hut. The bear slept with the dogs and came out to play and to be hand fed by the woman of the house. After three years they would kill the bear as a sacrifice to the masters of the taiga. Special dishes were carved with the image of a bear's head and chains made with real links.[4] Some of the dishes had the form of a dipper. Other dishes had the design of a dragon or snake – this is the sky god, the most powerful of all deities. People prepared many wood streamers from willow, alder, and bird cherry.[5] These were used to cleanse the bear from evil spirits and allow new flesh to grow. When the people eat, the spirits of their deceased relatives are fed at the same time, and they are happy.

Two men would guide the bear on two chains around an ice hole in the river. It is a good omen if the bear takes a drink. Then they went along a corridor of poles with wood streamers on them, about one kilometre to the place called *arachu*, prepared for the killing. Women played special rhythms on a musical instrument made of a hollow log.[6] The women dance the part of the bear.

The men take the bear to the house of the person who is hosting the feast. The bear crosses the threshold three times – if he crosses with two paws it means he is not offended and wishes well to the family. Then they go back to the place of sacrifice. First they shoot three arrows in the air – to the earth, the sky, and the taiga – and then the last arrow to the bear's heart.

Mourning begins in the family. There are special rituals for taking off the skin – each male must touch the skin to get a blessing on his future success as a hunter. There was a big celebration with singing, feasting and sports events. Afterward the bones were wrapped and placed in another special little house. ▼

In 1937 the ceremony was to be hosted by Nadezhda Duvan's family. But at the last minute the authorities arrived, "arrested" the bear, and took him away on a steamship!

Nadia noticed that Ycha had a wooden amulet hanging over the end of the metal bed-frame. "Do you divine?" she asked.

"Nu," said Ycha. (It had taken me a while to learn that this neutral speech particle actually means yes in this kind of situation.) She took the amulet down and listened to our questions: would Nadia get an apartment? Had my house sold? Slowly, pendulum-like, the amulet began to move. Nadia would get the apartment but not soon. The house had not sold – it was too expensive. Both turned out to be true. A year later Nadia had received the right to an apartment in a building that was not complete, construction halted for lack of funds. A year later my house finally sold for a low price. Four years later Nadia at last moved into the apartment.

By now Ycha had remembered a story. She told it in the Ul'chi language while we recorded it on tape and later that evening Mado translated it into Russian.

TWO SISTERS

Two sisters lived together. The younger sister had a small child. One day the older sister said, "Let's go over to the island and pick rose-hips. Look, they are growing way over there."

"No, I don't see any over there," said the younger sister.

"Well, go around the island and look and you'll find some."

She went to look, and when she came back she saw her older sister take the cradle with her little son and throw it right in the water!

Fishskin clothing, made from the skin of a sheat-fish,
in the Bulava museum.

She started to cry, "What are you doing? Why did you do that? Why did you kill my son?" And as she cried, she fell into a faint. She was in that kind of shape.

A goat approached her. He licked her and licked her. She said, "Don't lick me while I'm alive. Wait until I am dying and then lick me."

And then she started to die.

That woman said, "Now I am dying, lick me with your saliva. First my face."

The goat licked her face and she started to come to life.

"And my hands." Her hands came to life.

"And my feet." Her feet came back to life.

"Now my body." And when the goat licked her body, she came back to life completely. "You have saved me and now I won't die."

"Now let's go away from this place," said the goat.

They went a long way away, came to a house, and started to live there. They lived well, in a friendly way, but then the woman started to notice that the goat often went away somewhere. He'd go away in the evening and come back in the morning.

The woman was curious and she asked, "Why, goat, do you go away in the evening and come back in the morning? I won't tell you what you should or shouldn't do. But please, don't hide anything from me."

"I go over to the island," he said. "A boy comes up out of the water and I play with him. It's fun there with him. I tell him stories."

"That must be my son, the one my sister threw into the water in his cradle. She envied me. I want to see my son. I would like to bring him back."

"That will be very hard, because others have brought him up, there in the water," said the goat.

She started to prepare special foods, cereal, dried fish called *yukola*, everything. "This food will help me to bring my son back." And she left that food along the way to the island, all the way over there.

There she hid, and the goat called, "Child, come out. We'll play, I'll tell you stories …"

And from the water the child said, "I'm afraid, there's something bad out there."

"No, don't be afraid, there's nothing wrong."

"All right," said the boy, and he came out. They played together and then the goat started to trick him.

"Look, there's something tasty here on the ground." The child tasted the food his mother had left and said, "Mmm, this is good, there's something familiar about it." And so they tricked him and he came along until he got to the threshold of the house. When he got there he said, "Oh I remember, when I was little this is the way my mother's milk tasted." They closed the door and that woman tore her clothes, sobbed, and threw herself to her child.

But suddenly the child began to cry. "My mama is salmon and sturgeon my father. Mama and Papa, I love you!" It turns out it was the mother salmon and father sturgeon who had brought him up in the water. They were his adoptive parents.

When those fish started to come up out of the water to take back their child, the woman killed them. After that the mother started to live with her son.

But then she got very sick. It seemed that she had not been forgiven by the god for her sin in killing the adoptive parents of her child. And now she got really sick.

The goat said, "I had three souls. One I gave up when I saved you, the second I gave up when I was taking care of the child, and the third when I brought him here. Now all that's left for me to do is to die. Don't cry, but when I die, take my skin, sleep on it and cover yourself. And don't cry."

And then the goat died, and they did everything as promised, and she and the child slept on the skin and covered themselves with it. She got well and was happy with her child.

And that's the end. ▼

As in the stories of the Ice Mountain and Yegdyga and the Seal,[7] saliva heals wounds. The story also reminds me of Anna Khodzher's tale of Endohochen,[8] where the horse sacrificed his life and the girl slept with her child in the skin. But this story has a second part. Ycha went on.

The child grew up and started to shoot from the bow. His mother gave him very strict instructions. "You can shoot up the Amur and down the Amur but never never shoot across to the other side. That I forbid."

And so he shot up and down and at the same time he was curious. Why did his mother forbid him? And one time he couldn't resist, but shot over to the other side. His arrow didn't stop in one place but jumped here and there. Finally it stopped beside some kind of crack in the ice. It was beside a house.

Out of the house came an old man. "Who are you?" he asked.

"Oh, I just happened to come here," said the boy.

"Come visit us."

So he went in.

The house was awful; messy and dirty. But what could he do? The woman prepared something and it tasted very bad. She prepared it and gave it to him but he didn't eat it, he just pretended to eat it. His mother had fed him very well; everything was tasty and good. He threw bits of the food here and there, trying not to offend them. But they could see that he didn't like it, that it tasted bad.

Then they decided to lie down to sleep. The bedding was very nasty, torn and dirty. He lay down and pretended to sleep but in fact he didn't sleep.

The old man said, "Tell me a story."

The boy really didn't like it in that house, but he thought, just so as not to make them angry, not to show that he didn't like it, he'd start to tell. At the same time he was slowly and quietly getting dressed. He told further and got into his pants, further and he put on his jacket, then shoes and hat.

Little by little the old people closed their eyes, thinking that he was asleep there. He got one foot over the threshold, a second foot … and … ran for it! He realized that this man was his father. He ran and ran.

The old man also guessed that this was his son and ran after him calling, "Stop, stop, I'm your father."

The boy ran and ran and at last got to the shore where his mother lived.

He ran into the house and she was waiting, "I told you not to shoot over to that other side," she said. "Hurry up and come in."

They shut the door and the old man started knocking, "I'm your father. Wife, forgive me, let me in."

"No, I won't let you in. Only when you bring me the eye of my older sister, then I will let you in."

What could he do? He ran away. He brought an eye.

"Here is your sister's eye."

"Let me look at it."

She threw it there to the window in the ceiling, and then said, "No, that is not the eye of my sister. That's a dog's eye. Until you bring me my sister's eye, I won't let you in."

He ran away again and this time he brought another eye.

"Let me look," she said. She checked the eye, she threw it up to the light. It was turning this way and that, looking all around. She said, "Yes, that is my sister's eye."

It was like an evil eye. She broke that eye up, so that it wouldn't bother anyone else. And then she let him in.

The boy said, "Mama, let papa in, he loves us." So she let him in. And he wanted to embrace her. She wouldn't let him. But the son said, "Mama, let him embrace you." And at last she took pity on him and he embraced her. And so they were reunited.

That's the story! ▼

As in Anna Khodzher's "Puppy" tale, there is a story within a story. Again the child reunites the family through
telling the difficult truths. This story also probably reflects
a hunting taboo about crossing a river. On the other hand,
in Amur cultures, as in many other parts of the world, crossing a river is a metaphor for death. Like Anna Khodzher's
"Boy Who Went to a Forbidden Place," this boy disobeys his
mother and opens the family to transformation.

Ycha's granddaughter, folklorist Irina Rosugbu, writes
about the power of the eye in connection with Ulchi dolls.
She learned that toy dolls do not have eyes because adding
that detail would bring the doll to life, taking it out of the
realm of children's play. A shaman's *sevéns*, on the other
hand, which are understood to be living beings, do have
eyes – these are the last details to be added, thus enspiriting
the figure.[9]

I wanted to visit shaman Sophia Anga, who had been
described by Nadezhda Duvan. She was then about eighty-
five years old and still maintained an active practice. But the
time didn't seem right just yet. And the time must be right
for visiting a shaman, especially an unknown one.

First we went to see Chana Marfan, another grandmother on Mado's list. Her house was a contrast to Ycha's, warm
and noisy with grand-children. Chana's daughter gave us
fried potatoes and tea.

Chana described her earliest memory of a shaman.

MEMORIES OF A SHAMAN

When I was very little, a shaman came from another village to make things better. She walked all the way around
the village, gathering people, wearing wood streamers and
a shaman's belt. Many of the most respected people had
known she was coming in advance and made the streamers. Everybody gathered and held on, one behind the

Chana Marfan with her family.

other. She walked and sometimes ran. I held on to the leather strap at the very end, since I was small. I was interested. I fell down and then got up and ran again. The shaman knew it. Either someone told her or she just knew it. They prepared Labrador tea (ledum), cups and water, and poured it onto our house. She sat down to shamanize. She was brought there for a special purpose. She said my spirit had been taken – she breathed it back in at the top of my head. It was a cold feeling, as if my skull opened up. I'll never forget it. It happened long ago, before my first menstruation. I'll never forget it."9 ▼

When Chana married, her husband's family came and took her away in a boat. She had all her things packed in a trunk, including Chinese silk. She still had the trunk and wanted parts of it to be included in her grave, in spite of the fact that much of it has rotted.

After we finished eating our potatoes, Chana's oldest daughter, Katia, sat with us listening. After Katia's birth, for the following sixteen years all Chana's babies died. This time she called shaman Anga who told her, "You should not call this man papa but uncle." Anga came to the pregnant Chana just before birth. She discovered that the souls of the children had been stolen and she breathed them back into the mother's head. She flew away to find them. Then the mother had to keep her head covered for several days. After that five more live children were born. Again Chana described the sensation of her skull opening and the cold feeling as the shaman breathed the souls back in. Although divorce was unusual at that time, Chana later divorced her husband because he drank. It is possible that his drinking endangered the children's souls and for that reason Anga had recommended moving him to the more distant relationship of uncle.

Researcher Anna Smolyak told me that Nanai shamans had a special place where they kept the souls of vulnerable children, watching over them as if they were in a kind of spiritual nursery. This place was usually in a cliff at the base of a mountain. Ul'chi acquaintances confirm that their own children have personal shamans who keep their souls in a place whose location even the mother does not know. Smolyak says that the shaman does a ritual to return the soul permanently when the child is anywhere from ten to twenty years old, or sometimes at the time of marriage.[11]

We checked in at the museum, where the children were dressing for their performance. The museum itself is worth careful attention, brand new and decorated with intricate wood carvings by Kolya U and other artists. It is full of historical material, *sevéns*, fishskin coats, and embroidery.

Ul'chi barn, now in the Bulava regional museum. Barns were built on stilts to reduce incursions by mice.

Ul'chi barn door with carved design, Bulava museum.

It turned out the cruise ship was not coming that day after all. Mado was disgusted but the children's spirits were not dampened.

Our next step was to talk with Anga. We found her alone at her house. She had a roomer, who some said was her lover, but he was not home. We came in and sat down. I gave her some American cigarettes.

First she divined the answers to some of our personal questions by asking her "god," a wooden figure that looks either like a person with wings or a bird. Other such divination figures resemble snakes or tigers. The figure used for divination is suspended on a leather string and moves in response to questions put by the shaman. Before asking questions Anga breathed tobacco smoke onto the figure. Her answers were even more penetrating than Ycha's. Besides answering questions about love and Nadia's ever-present apartment question, she saw that Nadia had shamanic ancestry, as in fact she does. To me she said, "You too are not an ordinary person. Among your ancestors there were also people like me – you see things others do not see." After this, she told us the story of her own ancestry.

THE SHEAT-FISH

Mama was a Yakut. I am a Yakut daughter, not pure Gilyak.[12]

There were many sheat-fish. People were killing them. My ancestor was scared. She looked out. "What is making the noise?" That sheat-fish, waving his tail, came over the threshold.

She was scared. There was war with Japan at that time. The men in her family had been killed. She was alone with no firewood, no water. She wanted to eat but was scared to go out. She dozed and then the fish said, "Don't be scared. I came so that we could be husband and wife." She was scared. She had no water and wanted to eat. All

Ul'chi shaman Sofia Anga. She wears formal Ul'chi attire for
ceremonies, instead of a traditional shaman's costume.

day she went hungry. He was still there, blocking the threshold.

"All right," he says, "step over me, bring wood and water, cook and eat." She dozed again and he says, "Eat and lay down to sleep. I came so you will be my wife." She went to sleep and when she woke up a man was there. She gave birth to a son. That fish stayed in the form of a human being. So they lived and lived together.

Then one day he said, "We'll go somewhere far away, along the Amur. We've lived here and we still don't know how people live on the Amur. Let's go and live there. Our children will grow up."

They arrived and gave birth to my mother's mother and to me. I am a Yakut. That's how it is.

My mama told me that story one time. We were little then. Now giving birth is easy. You don't have to go anywhere, to a special birth hut. My mama couldn't rest. In those days you gave birth and three days later went out fishing.

Our grandfather was an old man and he educated us. This day we went across the Amur in a boat. We children were crying. There was a sheat-fish there, big and shining. We saw one boat turn over.

My grandfather said, "That's not a boat but a fish-person. They swallow boats." At that time mama had not told us the story of her ancestor. A little later, we saw one of the fish again.

My sister-in-law was Nanai. She said, "Is that a motorboat or not?" We were on our way to Mongol village because my cousin's sister had died. "Oh, what a boat!" she said.

"No, it's not a boat but a sheat-fish. They swallow boats," said my grandfather. I ran away. We went to a dry place and sat there waiting. We didn't know what to do. We threw all our cigarettes as offerings into the water, until none was left. We sat.

He was this big! Then he dove and was gone. We

waited. I was pale as pale. Mama said, "What is the matter? Are you sick?" I told what I had seen and then mama told me the story of how we were born. "You need to pray to the god," she said.

We arrived safely and mama said, "Pray to the god."[13] ▼

Seeing the big fish on the Amur seems to have triggered an ancestral memory or a vision for Anga, which prompted her mother to tell her this legend about her origins. In itself the story follows the familiar pattern of marriage with an animal or fish, but it purports to be set closer to the present time than most mythic tales, which gives it greater credibility to Anga's listeners.

Our next visit to Anga followed a lengthy search for a bottle of vodka for her spirits, difficult to find on a rainy Sunday because the store was closed. We had gone back and forth the length of the village following misleading directions to the homes of bootleggers with no success – probably because we were both unknown in Bulava. Tired and soaked to the skin, we went back to Anga and offered her money to buy the vodka herself. She agreed.

This time Anga took out her drum and put on her belt and a headdress made of wood shavings. She drummed and sang a prayer for good weather and for the health and happiness of the children. She prayed that there would be many shamans in the future.

"May the rain go away a little. How can we feed the children if everything rots in the gardens? Let us have sun."

Anga sang right into the back of the drum. She waved the front flaps of her robe to clear the weather. She said it would be impossible to drum without singing. She used two sets of wood streamers, waving them in front of the client, to determine whether or not she would be able to work shamanically for them. At the end of her drumming she took off the heavy belt and hit herself over the back with it, crossing both shoulders. This was to cleanse herself. Although the belt was very heavy, she said it did not hurt.

The next day the weather cleared up.

Anga's drum has been passed down from her grandfather to her father to her, but now she was not certain whom to pass it to.

She then told us how she became a shaman. (I had heard this story before, in the summer of 1994 in the United States, as told by Anga's neighbour, Nadezhda Duvan.)

HOW ANGA BECAME A SHAMAN

At the age of nineteen Anga saw several dreams. In them her father taught her to be a shaman. In her childhood she had dreamed several times that she was living with the tiger. She gave birth to three baby tigers but wouldn't agree to raise them and instead gave them to the tiger-father. When she was grown up, again she had the dream of living with the tiger and this time she gave birth to two baby tigers. She kept them with her. During journeys she now rides on the tigers. Her helping spirit is *Duse*, the flying tiger. Its image has wings and a person on the back with the face of a bear. She goes through the lower, middle, and upper worlds.

At twenty years of age, she dreamed of flying to the lower world, over the ocean. There were seven mountains with fire burning. The tiger came to her and became her spirit, holding her there. To get free she got help from her grandmother, a shaman, who helped bring her spirit back. After that she stopped getting sick. To get to the upper world she goes through the larch tree, she goes through the clouds. She sees an opening. Around the opening are seven girls with mallets in their hands. There is a huge space and a statue the size of a house. This statue is a Manchurian god.

Anga suffered from ages nine to seventeen. She was very sick but had to see it through. She stopped getting sick after her grandmother-shaman helped her to escape. Ever since that time the spirits have forced her to drum." ▼

Listening to Duvan, I had interpreted the story of marriage with the tiger as happening in another reality – as a vision. The story as Anga told it to us in her own home now was much the same but the response was different. Since I had heard the story before I listened with anticipation but without too much surprise. Nadia, on the other hand, was truly astonished and questioned many points. It seems possible from the following story that Anga had gotten pregnant from being scratched by the tiger.

We were looking at a woollen wall-hanging in the image of a lion on her wall, which turned the conversation back to tigers. Anga explained that the tiger shows her how to make amulets of hay.

Nadia asked, "Do you dream of the tiger?"

"The tiger helps me when shamanizing," Anga replied.

THE TIGER HUSBAND

Long ago my tiger husband came along the road. He was so big. He came up in front of the door and looked in. He went along until he came to a village by Marinsk, to the very end of the village and then up. The tiger came to a house and made his own separate house nearby. "Why don't you go on?" they asked. He went around the house three times and then went on.

He came to where I lived, but we were all covered with deep snow. That's why he made his house separately in the taiga. He crossed three mountains to come here. There was deep water, like a well. He washed off all the dirt. He washed three times and after the third time he was shining.

When I was little the tiger slept with me. He was like a big fur coat! I slept like the dead. I didn't tell mama.

My father scared the tiger and he ran away. My father said, "She will be a shaman." He made a wooden tiger and shamanized. "The tiger scratched you, that's why you cried," he said.

I got pregnant. I came to a place where there was nobody, just some old woman I met there. I cursed. Three tiger babies were born. I was mad and threw them right at the tiger. "I don't need these, I need my own." The tiger took them away. ▼

"Is this true?" asked Nadia.

"Yes. Again I got pregnant. He came at night. This time I had two tiger babies. One sat on each of my knees and they put their paws on my shoulders. They wanted to suck my breasts, one here and one here. This time I said to the father, 'I won't give you these. Go away.' He went away."

"Where did the tiger babies go?"

"They are alive, they help me."

"Are they in the taiga?"

"They are here with me. You don't see them?"

"No."

"I see them."

"Do you have human children?"

"No, I can't."

"Do you have grandchildren?"

"Probably, but you shouldn't ask too much about shaman's business! Another time I saw a dream. I was hunting and went far away. I came to a place where there were two houses close together. I had to decide which one to go into. I went into one and dishes were set out there, the kind you use for offering food and praying to the god. There was one wooden god there. I looked at her. Then I turned and when I looked back she was crying. A baby tiger was running there."

In retrospect I wonder if Anga had miscarriages in the human world. Our conversation continued on the subject of tigers. Anga told this story about her grandfather.

ANGA'S GRANDFATHER AND THE TIGER

My mother's father was out hunting. One day he came back to the hunting tent and found a female tiger there. He was about to shoot but didn't. He put down his gun. He dozed and then slept.

The tiger spoke to him, "I am a tiger woman. Lie down with me and sleep. I will live with you. Eat what is in the bowl." He ate, gave the bowl back, and slept. They lived as husband and wife. He lived with her for three years. She said, "Take all your traps." She showed him how to set them near the house. In the morning he cleaned them out and they were always full.

He came there in the fall, lived through the winter, and in the spring set off to go home. When he left, she told him not to wear a certain pair of boots that had been made for him at home in his absence.

"They have a bad smell. If you wear them I will take you away completely," she said. He went home, but he forgot what she had said. He put on the boots and died. They found marks on his body that looked like a tiger, with the head and tail coming around his waist – like a sore in the shape of a tiger. ▼

Although told about a person Anga remembers, the story contains the common folktale motif of forgetting what one has been told in the world of spirit. Another shamanic theme is the spacious play with time – did the man stay three years or one winter with the tiger-woman? And how was this time experienced by his relatives? In some tales a person returns home from a meeting with otherworld beings to find that many years have gone by and all his relatives have died. On the other hand a shaman may describe a journey of many years that takes place in a ceremony lasting a few hours.

Ul'chi children on the bus going to perform traditional dances
at a regional festival.

That evening we discussed Anga's stories with Mado. Is it possible that a human woman really married a tiger and gave birth to tiger children? Mado said it could be possible, although it could also be a vision.

She told about another female shaman she knew, who now lived in another village.

TWO GIRLS WHO MARRIED TIGERS

In her childhood this woman had two sisters who disappeared into the taiga for several months. When they came back they looked completely healthy and well. They got right to work, sewing and embroidering wedding clothes for themselves. They said they were leaving for good. The father cried. When they were ready, the girls took their things and left the house.

The little girl watched through a needle hole in the
fishskin window as they walked toward the woods. She saw
two big tigers come out. The girls got on their backs and
disappeared. That little girl grew up to be a powerful
shaman. She is the one people consult most often today
when something really serious happens. ▼

Marriage with tigers was being entertained as a real possibility, not a vision. It seemed all the more possible in
Anga's case because she had no human children. This is a
difficult problem for folklorists and ethnographers who
enter a culture different from their own – how to relate to
things that seem impossible and yet are accepted as literal
truth. The generation to which Mado and Nadia belong is
in something of a middle position – they live in close prox-
imity to the older generation, the last to fully understand
the older way of life and its underlying philosophy, and at
the same time they have been educated in schools that
taught atheism. All agree that shamanism is an area that
should not be examined too closely – either from respect
for the elders or because of the dangers involved in a close
examination of the shamanic world.

The next day we bounced over a dirt road by bus to the
nearby town of Bogorodskoe where the children were to
perform for national television at a holiday celebration on
the beach. The children sang all the way and shared their
food in a way I found remarkable. They almost competed in
giving things away. "Who will eat some of my tomatoes?"
"Take some of my potatoes!" Clearly they had been brought
up with less emphasis on possessions than many North
American children.

But after we arrived at the beach it began to rain, things
were late starting, and by the time the boat races and wood-
chopping competitions finished, there was no time for the
children to perform. They were goodnatured about this too
and spent the day picking mushrooms and playing on the
beach.

On my last day in Bulava I met two more storytellers. The first was Nina Vasilievna Munina. She lived over the hill in Old Bulava. Her husband was building them a new house and she was asleep in the old one while her grandson watched television. We waited outside in some embarrassment for her to wake herself up, wondering if she were ill or perhaps had been drinking. But eventually she called us into the house. She sang several songs in honour of the river, called by its Ul'chi name, Mangbo, or powerful place.

Then she told this story. I was thrilled to hear it, as it is a different version of one of my favourite stories to tell. It is about a form of male initiation and again involves a tiger. She told it in Ul'chi and then translated it herself.

THE BOY AND THE TIGER

In one settlement there lived an old man and an old woman. They had a son. One time the old man went hunting and took his son with him. He brought firewood to the hunting camp, boiled tea, and made a little sacrifice to the spirits.

The son went hunting with his father. They came back to the hut in the evening, made tea, and rested. They lay down to sleep. I don't know how long they slept but the father saw a dream.

Amba, the tiger, said to the father, "Old man, leave me your son here, don't take him with you. If you take him with you I will come and kill you both."

The man woke up and thought and thought about what to do, tears in his eyes. He was sorry to leave his son. "But I can't take him either, because if I do the tiger will kill us both. My wife is at home – how will she live alone without us? Want to or not, I have to leave my son."

He sat up quietly, without waking his son, he kissed him gently, he wept, and then crawled out of the tent. He went away. He walked and walked toward home and when he got close the dogs started to bark, greeting him.

His wife came out. She asked, "Where is our son? Why have you come alone?" She asked several times, "Where have you left our son?"

He was silent – he couldn't say anything. She asked several times and at last he had to tell her everything. He told about his dream, how the tiger had said to leave his son, how he said if you don't leave him I will kill you both.

"I saw a dream," said the father, "where the tiger said, 'if you don't leave your son I will kill you both. And if you go home alone, I won't.' I thought and thought and finally left our son."

Of course she started to cry, she cried loudly. She said, "Of course it is a shame just to leave a small child like that." And so she cried and then they went home together and went in.

The father stayed there and now we will go back to the taiga. The boy is sleeping, turning this way and that. He wakes up and it is already light. He looks around and his father is not there.

He woke up quickly, got up and went to the door. He looked out and saw that his father was not there anywhere. Then he saw a big tiger, coming out of the taiga. Terrible! The boy was frightened. He ran away to a big old tree, and climbed up high. The tiger came after him. He came to the tree and started to climb. He broke one branch, and then another.

The tiger got caught in the branches and couldn't move one way or the other. Using his strap, the boy jumped down to the ground and looked around to see what to do next.

The tiger was begging, "Son, my son, help me, take pity on me." His tears were flowing. "Help me – cut this tree and I will do everything for you that you want. I'll make it so that you will live in wealth."

All right, so the boy ran to the tent, took up his little axe, ran back and started chopping. He chopped and

chopped and chopped all day – after all, he was only a little boy. Finally, somehow, he managed to cut off the part
of the tree that was holding the tiger and the tiger fell to
the ground with a great roar!

He looked at the boy, turned and somehow stumbled
off into the taiga. He hid himself. The boy went back into
the tent, made himself some tea, and then fell asleep and
saw a dream.

In his dream the tiger said, "You helped me. So I will
help you. Tomorrow take your traps, go and set them and
use your sleeve to wipe away your tracks from around the
traps. Do it like that."

In the morning the boy got up and took everything the
tiger had said to take. He went and set the traps. He wiped
away the snow with his sleeve and went back. Then the
second morning he went and looked and saw that he had
caught so many sable! Every trap was full.

He took them and went home to the tent. He prepared
them, hung the skins up to dry. Every day he hunted like
that and every day he got many sable. He filled the whole
tent.

All right, now let's leave him there and go back to the
shore. The boy's father said to his mother, "I guess I'll go
and see if he is alive or not. If he has died, I will bring
back his bones. If he is alive, I'll bring him and we'll come
back together."

His wife said, "Of course father, go, see if he is alive or
dead." So the father got ready, dressed and set off. He
walked and walked. And as he got close to the tent he saw
smoke coming from it.

"He must be alive," the father thought.

He walked faster, opened the door and looked inside.
There sat his son on the bench. When he recognized his
father, the boy jumped to his neck, and they embraced.

The boy showed how much fur he had, he told everything that had happened.

They took it all, tied it to the sleigh, went home, and

Ul'chi embroidered coat, Bulava museum.

they live there, getting richer, to this very day.

I'm joking! ▼

The fact that the storyteller repeats the tiger's threat four times proves that the man was justified in leaving his son. I enjoyed Nina's technique of moving from the shore to the taiga as if she were turning the lens of a camera, using changes in verb tense for emphasis.

Many versions of this story appear in books. Often the tiger takes the boy on his back all the way to the top of the mountain. There he takes off his tiger skin and turns into a man. The tiger-man's family reward the boy for sparing their son, who teaches him how to hunt. In one version the son spends the night with the tiger people and awakens in the night to the raucous sound of a houseful of tigers snoring! The next day he goes home laden with sableskins. In this initiation tale the hunter receives aid from the master of the taiga, as do many shamans.

That evening Mado took us to meet one last storyteller – Grandma Nyura, or Anna Alexeevna Kavda. She was born in Bulava in 1925. Mado listened to her stories in Ul'chi with great care and affection, clarifying what Nyura meant about various words and ideas. When we got home she translated the stories from the tape.

THE SWAN GIRLS

There lived two brothers. They were orphans, they had no parents. They lived as they could. The older brother was very strong. He fished and hunted. The younger brother was lazy, he lay around at home all the time. The older brother brought him fish. In the forest he shot animals and brought meat.

One time the older brother was away and the younger was at home alone. They lived on top of a hill. The one who was at home saw seven swans. They came flying to earth beside his house, took off their feathers, and turned into seven girls.

The girls came into the house, they cleaned everything up beautifully, and then they started to sew beautiful clothes for that younger brother. Then they searched his head for lice, washed his head, and flew away. They turned back into swans.

The older brother came home from hunting, looked around, saw how clean everything was and thought, "Can my younger brother have done all this?" There he was, all clean and dressed up in beautiful clothes. He had all kinds of clothes, for hunting, for fishing, for holidays – everything, including shoes.

"Who did all this?" he asked.

The younger brother told him everything that had happened.

The older brother said, "If this happens again, let's try to catch them. You stay here and I'll hide in the *chongo*." In the Ul'chi homes there was an air space up above, called *chongo*. "I'll hide there. I'll turn into a fly and sit there as quiet as can be. When they go to fly away we will try to catch them, the two of us. We'll take them as wives."

"Fine, let's try," said the younger.

The older brother turned into a fly and hid in the air space.

The swan girls flew up, they came in and worked. They sewed the older brother all kinds of clothes, for everyday, for holidays, everything.

Then that younger brother complained that everything itched – and so they cleaned up his head. And then they got ready to fly away. And again he complained that something itched, so as not to let them go.

Then that older brother turned back into a man and boom! He fell onto the floor.

The girls were frightened. Somehow they got into their swan clothes and started to fly away. But the brothers caught two of them, who became their wives.

The other girls turned into swans who cried and flew around that house crying "Kila-a kila-a, how will we fly away without you?"

And then they flew away.

The brothers and their wives started to live well, in wealth. The older brother was very strong. He was called Natalka.

Then what? He went away and found those other sisters and brought them back. It was very difficult, he had to fight, there were evil spirits there. The sisters were all in different places but the wives showed the brothers where to look. At last he found all the sisters, brought them back, and they all lived together. Afterwards he built a big house, with one half for Natalka and the other for his brother. ▼

The word *kilaa* means swan in Ul'chi, similar to *kilae*, the seagull, in Udegei. Mado says that stories like this explain the custom of men having several wives. Certain parts of the story are sung – those are important conversations. The swan girls reminded me of the Nivkh tale of the "Knee Bump" where the young man also marries a girl who arrives in the form of a swan. The swan is a sacred bird, having the ability to fly in the upper world and dive to the underwater world while living in the middle world.

The other story Nyura told reminds me of Valentina Kyalundzyuga's tale of the man who married a seal, and Maria Beldi's "Girl in the Ice." It was shortened in the telling because Nyura was getting tired.

THE TAIMEN GIRL

A young man fell in love with a girl and that girl had many sisters. They were taimen fish. The fish turned into girls and this young man came down to the shore and admired them. He fell in love with one of them.

They started to eat together and play. At first his mother didn't know. The mother was a nasty woman and she followed her son, she really didn't want him to ... well, after all, the girl was a fish!

The mother wanted to kill that taimen-girl. She wounded her with a knife. There was a lot of blood and the fish just barely managed to swim away. All the taimen swam away.

After that the young man, Mergen, who had fallen in love, decided to find his fish-girl. He started to look for her under the water. As he searched, they called to each other and that is the musical part of the story. "Where are you, my Pudi, my beauty? I'm looking for you."

She answered, "I'm far away, I'm dying."

That mother was a nasty woman, she sent some kind of magic people after him who made metal sabres and things like that – she was like a witch. She tried to make it so that her son would not find the girl. The road was very bad, scary and difficult.

The mother turned into various things, a duck for one. The young man had many adventures but in the end he found his girl.

In the end, he saw a girl carrying a basin of blood. He sang to her. She poured the blood onto her sister. There were nine sisters and eight carried blood to save the other. He went to each village and everywhere the sisters brought blood in birch-bark containers. They brought it and poured it on the wound. In each place he asks, "Tell me where she is. Please, help me find her."

And they answer, "Go further."

His brothers and father also wanted to prevent him from marrying a fish. Apparently there was a taboo against a man of the land marrying like that. The father and brothers started to smith iron weapons to kill that Mergen.

At last he won and they gave their permission. They all surrendered to him and he took all the girls home. In the

end he won his own with the force of his love. They could-
n't do anything more and he took all the girls home with
him. All the sisters fell in love with him and wanted to live
with him. He became a hero. ▼

8

Nanai Storytelling in Nizhnye Khalby and Kondon

Nadia and I visited several more villages on the river, travelling on the *Meteor* back upstream. Our first stop was Nizhnye Khalby, the home of other spectacular embroidery artists. We stayed with Svetlana Pavlovna Khodzher, who used to be a member of the Communist Party. She said her father was a shaman who worked quietly in the days when it was forbidden. His own wife forbade him to continue and eventually he gave his drum, belt and other shamanic equipment to the museum. His belt was very heavy, she remembers. The heavier the belt, the better it helped hold the shaman to the ground.

Svetlana Pavlovna's grandmother gave her a special leather bracelet with amulets on it that had protected her from illness all her life. Now her mother was keeping it to prevent Svetlana's becoming a shaman. Nadia laughed at a former party member believing such a thing. Svetlana smiled.

Nanai dress.

Next day I met the writer and historian Valentin Ilych Geiker. He has studied the history of the Nanai people extensively and remembers the tragedy when books in the Nanai language, printed in the Latin alphabet, were burned in the 1940s. All over the Soviet Union such books were destroyed during the changeover in language and educational policy that led to greater standardization and the almost exclusive use of Russian in schools.[1] He showed me the very place where the flames consumed those first Nanai works; ironically, it was just outside the school.

After claiming not to know any stories he told yet another version of frog and mouse that he learned from his grandmother, including the episode where frog races the moose. In his version mouse steals food from frog, both cherries and moose meat.

He also told the following historical legend about marriage with the tiger. Besides adding to my fund of tiger lore, this story recalls a time when only one person survives a disaster, as does Anna Khodzher's story of the Nanai violin. As in many other tales of marriage with animals, the resulting children are sacred twins, who carry on the clan. It is interesting that in this story the Nanai considered the tiger a relative before the birth of these children. As a historian, Valentin Ilych's main interest in the story was the explanation it provides for how the Geikers came to live so widely spread apart.

THE GEIKER CLANS

This was four, maybe five, maybe six hundred years ago. Our tribes were many; warlike tribes. Their neighbours were always afraid of them, our Geikers.

One time the enemies plotted together and attacked us at night. We lived in a big city, and there they killed everyone. They left neither children nor adults, nobody. Such moments happen in history.

Just one girl was left. She woke up, seriously wounded. She prayed to her god,[2] "Why was I left alone, one girl?" After all, even if she lives, she will marry another – she is not a carrier of the tribe. So why god left her was incomprehensible. She cursed god for leaving her alive. Better to have left a boy – he would have carried the Geiker clan on.

It happened that while she was crying, a tiger came out of the taiga and took her away into the forest. Time went by – it's not known whether it was two years or three, but she came out of the taiga and with her she had two babies, twins. The tiger's children, of course. And the two children grew. They got big and became excellent hunters. They brought back furs and meat.

Once an old tiger approached them in the taiga. This was in the winter. He came, spent the night by their camp, and in the morning went away. He kept watching them, following them. They thought they'd better get their mother's advice. According to the law of the taiga it was forbidden to kill a tiger. They were considered to be relatives to the Nanai people.

The mother realized that this tiger was the boys' father and decided to send them to a place where there were no tigers. She was afraid they would accidentally kill a tiger. And so she prepared her children for the road, gave each one a sled and dogs, clothing and food, and sent them down the river Sungari.

They came down river and when they got to the Amur they asked the people living there, "Are there tigers here? If there are none we will stop and live here." And they were told that it did happen that tigers came there, so they went further. And thus they came to the Anyui River – beside Naikhin village.

While they were on their way, winter ended, it was April and the ice in the Amur started to move. One of the twins said, "I'll go down and ask." And he got down from the ice and went to the settlement. And the second brother

Nanai *sevéns* in the Kondon museum.

stayed on the ice with the sleighs.

The moment the brother disappeared, the Amur moved. And so one brother went further down the Amur on the ice and the other stayed. They lost each other. And that's how it happened that they lived in different places. The other brother wound up around the contemporary village of Lower Tambov. There the great ice stopped and he got down. And there he built himself a house and later got married. And so one branch of the Geikers was there: Simasi, Kargi, Adi. Three Geiker villages. The other brother also married and had children and grandchildren. He made himself a separate settlement. And so both brothers lived and founded their Geiker settlements. That legend shows how it happened that there are Geikers both here and in that place. And I too am probably from there too, on my father's side. This story tells you about the constant movements of peoples. ▼

When the time came to leave Khalby, Svetlana took us down to the dock, warning that sometimes the *Meteor* doesn't stop here. The reason given is that the boat is already too full but people think there is a certain amount of racism involved. Nizhnye Khalby is a predominantly Nanai village, and the people on the *Meteor* may expect its inhabitants to get on the boat drunk. My observation is that this is equally if not more possible in a Russian village, but I remembered that when we arrived the boat had not come all the way to the dock and certainly had not tied up. We were shoved across the gap, and the boat took off before anyone could get on. And in fact while we waited on the dock, the *Meteor* passed us by.

This was not a huge problem, said Svetlana – another boat, the *Rocket*, would come soon. She had come down yesterday and told the drivers that important American guests who had to catch the plane to Moscow would be getting on. Obviously former party members know how to get things done! The *Rocket* stopped and we got on.

From Komsomolsk-na-Amure we went inland to the Nanai village of Kondon. I had read about Kondon, which is the site of interesting archaeological digs. In the nineteenth century the village was very wealthy and their men went into China to trade sable for silks, jewellery, guns, and other goods. In Nergen in 1993 we had seen gorgeous Chinese silk coats that Violetta Khodzher's family had brought from Kondon. Unfortunately the Kondon museum has now been robbed of most of its valuables.

You can get to Kondon on the train. We were told to buy a ticket for Harpichan station, which we did. The piece of information we missed was that you had to request that the train stop a few kilometres before Harpichan and let you out! The village is a 1.5 kilometre walk from where the train stops.

Inside the train was sweltering. We were happy to get off at Harpichan, which is on the Baikal-Amur mainline. The mainline was built some years back when the Soviet Union was on bad terms with China and feared that the trans-Siberian railway ran too close to the border with China for comfort. They built a new route, complete with beautiful stations with marble floors and pillars – and then went on using the old route for long-distance passengers and freight. The station at Harpichan may be beautiful, but it was closed up tight. A bus was waiting to pick up the other passengers who got off – but it was not going to Kondon. A man pointed down a rough track, saying Kondon was that way.

We set off walking. Our bags were heavy – Nadia's because people were always giving her things like litre jars of caviar and sacks of potatoes to take to other people, mine because it was full of presents for storytellers and people we stayed with. Theoretically my bag should have been getting lighter as we travelled; but the thing is that people also give me presents – often books …

The track soon ran into a swamp – and the mosquitoes found us. It didn't seem possible this was the right way, so we went back to the station, now with our feet wet. There was still nobody there.

This time we followed the road the bus had taken and soon came to a crossroads. We turned right, going parallel with the railroad tracks, vaguely in the direction the man had pointed. It was a long dusty walk to the next road, which eventually did lead to Kondon. The mosquitoes were still with us.

We finally arrived, tired, dusty, and bitten, and found the home of Lyubov Feodorovna Samar. When she heard what we had done, she couldn't stop laughing.

"No, no," she said, still laughing, "You buy the ticket for Harpichan and then get them to stop for Kondon. The railroad workers call it the rubber station! I can't believe you walked all that way – it's so far!"

I couldn't believe that the "rubber" station joke actually worked in both Russian and English. A crack began to form in my ill-humour.

Laughing is a way of life for Lyubov. Every story she told had us in gales of laughter, whether the subject was funny or not. There is something infectious about her humour as she told how she remembered hearing the tales as a child, laughing then as she did now.

THE FLEA DRUM

There once was a girl who lived alone. She decided to find herself a husband. She started to get ready and thought, "I'll look for a husband, but I need to think of something interesting, so I can tell who is the right one."

She made a drum and a drumstick. She got all dressed up, took the drum and the stick and went off whichever way her eyes fell first. She walked along and saw a house, there on the edge of the village. She went in and there lay a young man – really good looking! He was smoking a long clay pipe, resting after the hunt.

Contemporary Nanai wedding dress made by Lyubov Feodorovna
Samar, Kondon.

Contemporary Nanai wedding dress, made by Lyubov Feodorovna
Samar, back view. The lower panels show the tree of life. At the top
is the heavenly dragon.

Tree of life
embroidered by
Lyubov Samar.
The tree appears
on wedding dresses
because the birds
nesting in its
branches represent
the souls of the
bride's unborn
children.

Below: The heavenly
dragon Mudur
embroidered by
Lyubov Samar.

She came in and started to sing a shamanic song, and set him a riddle.

"Chikto chergee, chon chickie cho
 Soro-aa sorgee, chon chickie cho
 Neelo nergee, chon chickie cho.
 Chon chickie cho, chon chickie cho.

The fellow answered, "Do you really think that's a riddle? Of course I know what your drum and drumstick are made of. The drum is made of goat-skin and the drumstick is covered with dog fur."

The girl said, "You guessed wrong," and she went out, dancing and singing as she went. She went on and came to another settlement. And there on the edge of the settlement was a hut, even better than the first one.

She went in and there lay a young man, even better-looking than the first, smoking a long silver pipe.

She asked him, "Anda Merge, chon chickie cho. What is my drum made of and what is my drumstick made of?"

He answered, "What is there to guess? Your drum is made of goat-skin and the drumstick is covered with dog fur."

"You got it wrong," she said and went out, singing a song. She went on and came to another settlement. There she saw an even more beautiful house, decorated with gold and silver. She went in and there lay a young man who was absolutely good-looking! He was smoking a long gold pipe. He had a beautiful round face, like the sun.

She asked, "What is my drum made of and what is my drumstick made of?" He took his long pipe out of his mouth and said, "What is there to guess? The head of your drum is covered with the skin of a flea and the stick is covered with the skin of a louse."

And no sooner had he said that than her drum broke and the stick too! And that's how she found herself a husband!

And that's the end of the story.[3] ▼

196

Lyubov told the tale bilingually, in Nanai and Russian, moving from one language to the other with each repetition. The story is a kind of shamanic joke, which contains a deeper meaning. The girl is looking for a man who can see beyond the surface, just as she can herself. The breaking of her drum at the end could signify that she lost her shamanic power with marriage. Some people say that this was often the case with women shamans, but all the female shamans I have met have continued to practice throughout their child-bearing years.

The next tale is about Lakicho, who appears frequently in Nanai folklore according to Lyubov.

LAKICHO

Lakicho lived all alone. He had no relatives, but somehow he got along. Fall came, and with it the fish, the salmon. He went to the river and sang a song. He sang and sang and then a really big fish came to him. He grabbed the fish but the fish didn't want to come. He pulled and pulled and at last pulled it out. He cut the fish up, and made several barns full of *yukola*, or dried fish. He salted several barrels of fish and also cooked up some to eat. Then he sat there on the bed, smoking and thinking.

He thought, "How will I eat without teeth? I'll have to put in some iron teeth." But then he thought, "Iron teeth will bend. Better to use silver, but they too will probably bend." He thought and thought – and at last thought that it would be better make gold teeth. They won't break, nothing will go wrong with them.

While he was thinking, he heard a sound. There was someone outside the window. He looked and there was a bear.

"Aha, Lakicho," said the bear, "how are you living here? I see you've got all kinds of fish and caviar. I think I'll eat it all up. You don't even have one tooth, so how can you eat?"

Lakicho thought, "What can I do so that he won't eat it all up?" And he said, "Let me bring you a good knife. You can cut the fish up. Just wait here."

The bear was a little thick in the head; he said, "All right, I'll rest a little."

Lakicho went out and walked along the road thinking, "This is bad, I won't even get to eat a little of my fish." And on the way he met a fox.

The fox said, "Why are you crying, Lakicho?"

"I caught a big fish, dried it, salted it, and then a bear came along and is going to eat all my fish."

"That's a problem. I'll help you. When we get home, tell the bear that a hunter is coming. And lots of dogs, all barking. Say those hunters are going to kill him. And I will make a huge noise so he will really think hunters are coming."

Lakicho went home and woke the bear. "Mapa," he said, "Get up quickly! Hunters are coming, dogs are barking. They'll be here soon."

"Where can I hide? Any place I hide they will see me," cried the bear.

And Lakicho says, "Hide under this big *chan*, this iron pot. And when they have gone I will knock." So he hid him there behind the hearth and covered him with the *chan*.

Then the fox ran up to the window shouting, "Where is that bear? We hunters are going to shoot you." The bear was shaking with fright.

"Quick," said the fox to Lakicho, "Give me your axe." She took the axe and struck the pot, breaking it in two. She killed the bear. They cut the bear meat up and set up a great feast. They cooked up lots of food.

Then the fox said, "Lakicho, let's think of a game. Let's do this. First you tie me up and feed me with a spoon, and then I'll do the same for you. That will be really fun."

Lakicho was also a little thick in the head and he said, "Let's do it." He tied the fox, set her in the cradle and rocked her and fed her with a spoon.

"Now you feed me," he said after a while. Lakicho untied the fox and the fox tied him up really well. She took the spoon and waved it under his nose and then put the food right into her own mouth! She stuffed herself with everything there was to eat, left Lakicho there tied up. Then the fox ran away.

Lakicho lay there for a day, two days. He was dying of hunger, crying. "What am I going to do?"

Just then a mouse crawled out of a hole and started to run across Lakicho's body.

"Just don't eat me," said Lakicho, "I'm still alive. At least wait until I'm dead. Then you can eat me."

The mouse said, "I will help you. I will untie your ropes." And so she chewed through the ropes. Lakicho was so grateful that he patted the mouse, and then went out and shot a bird and brought the mouse food.

Then he said, "You stay here and guard the house. I'm going into the woods to find that fox, and then I will punish her."

He got dressed and went out.

After a while he came to one house. There were many foxes inside and they were singing and drumming shamanically. Among them he saw a familiar fox and at that very moment she was the one running with the drum.

"Now I'll catch her," he thought.

His fox saw him and got scared. She threw aside the drum and all the other shaman's things and hid in a corner. He pulled her out and took her outside.

"Now I'm going to punish you for everything, for the fact that I almost died of hunger. I will kill you and make your fur into a hat."

The fox said, "Oh, Lakicho, don't kill me. I will find you a wife, a beautiful one, hard-working, who will love you and give you lots of children."

"All right," said Lakicho, "if that's the way things are going, I agree. Just don't trick me."

"No, no, I won't trick you. Come with me."

This was in winter. You see, the other part was in the fall. He must have lain there hungry until winter.

They went along the snow and arrived at a village. At one house the fox said, "Wait here for me. An old man and woman live there and they have a daughter. Such a beauty, modest and hard-working! I will find a way so that she will marry you. Just wait for me."

The fox ran along, beside the river. Those people lived by the water. She crawled into a crack in the ice. The old man came out for water, and the fox grabbed him by the beard. The old man was frightened.

"Who's there? Evil spirits? *Amban*? Let me go."

Fox said, "I will not let you go. I'll only let you go if you go home and get your daughter all dressed, set her on a sleigh, and take her to the edge of the village and leave her there."

The old man thought it over. What could he do?

"All right," he said, "I will give you my daughter." He went home crying.

His daughter asked, "Why are you crying, papa?"

He told her what had happened. "Some devil in the ice crack grabbed me and made me promise to give you to him."

"Don't worry," she said. "Just do as he says. Put me on the sleigh and take me to the edge of the village."

And so he did. He took her on the sleigh to the edge of the village and left her there. Then the fox came out and said to Lakicho, "There she is, your bride. Grab her. Tie her sleigh with a rope and take her home."

They took her home. And that's how Lakicho found himself a wife. She turned out to be a good, hard-working person, but then after a while she started to look sad all the time.

"What's the matter with you?" he asked. "Why are you crying?"

"What can I do? You got me to marry you through trickery. And now my mama and papa are old. They've probably already gone blind from tears."

"I like you, I love you, we get along fine," said Lakicho. "Let's go get your parents and bring them back here."

And so they went and got the parents and they all lived together. That's the end of the story. ▼

Another tale recalls the theme of the girl who sleeps with something unusual that has turned up in her blanket. In these stories the girls instantly hide the thing they find, as if they know that a husband will emerge from it and that they will be the only ones to see him in his true from. The skull here represents the connection to the world of the ancestors. The story also contains a turnaround on the theme of testing the bride – here the girls' father tests the grooms.

THE GIRL AND THE SKULL

There lived two sisters, an older one and a younger. They lived separately from their parents, but the parents were not far away.

One day the younger sister went outdoors and hung up her blanket. And then she went inside. After a while she went out again and noticed that the blanket had fallen. There was no wind or anything. Why would the blanket fall? The dogs were tied up.

She took the blanket and shook it. Out fell a human skull! Without saying anything to her sister she wrapped the skull in the blanket, brought it home, and put it on her bed.

And so the skull stayed there to live with her. He slept with her at night. In the daytime she covered him. Time went by and the older sister noticed that the younger one was getting heavier, a belly showed on her for no apparent reason. She hadn't gone anywhere.

"What's this?" she thought. She went and told her parents. Papa came running.

"What's going on? From where? What's this?" And so she was forced to explain.

"This is what happened. I found the skull, brought him home, and now I've married him."

The older sister thought, "How can this be? Let's throw that skull out."

The younger sister started to cry. So they didn't throw it out but instead covered it with clay. This was during the day. She cried but there was nothing to be done. The parents made a scandal, they wanted to throw her out but she appealed to them and at last they agreed to let her live with her skull.

Then it came time for the other sister to get married. She found a human man, a good one, and the sisters started to live in separate houses. The one with her man and the other with her skull.

The younger gave birth to a baby, a good boy. And so they lived.

How did she live? She got up in the morning and went to her barn and there would be fresh fish and meat that had appeared during the night. She thought "How is this happening? The skull must be bringing it."

She watched one night and saw a fine young man coming out of the skull. A handsome Mergen. By morning he had brought back food. She started to think, wondering "Why do I only see him at night? I want to see him during the day."

One night when he was gone she took away that skull, encased in clay. And lay down to sleep. In the morning she woke up and there sat her husband. He was all blue-green from bad temper, smoking his long pipe. Right away she brought him food, but he remained silent. She did this, she did that, but he didn't react to anything.

Time went by, he smoked his pipe and then he said,

"You shouldn't have done that. My parents had many children and they all died young. I was the last to be born and the *dyuli*, (spirit figure) that protects our family made it so that in the day I would not appear before the eyes of people, but only at night. And now you have taken my protection."

She said, "I'll give it back. I just want to see you a little bit in the light." They agreed on this, she gave him back his skull.

Then her father came to visit and said, "You're living with your skull. Your sister has a fine hunter and brings us food. Let's arrange a competition to see who is the better hunter. I see that you are eating meat but I have never seen your man. Let him show himself. We'll have a competition to see who kills more wild animals. Tell your husband."

And he left.

They came together, the skull-man and the other sister's husband. Skull went first, at night. He got on his skis. Along the way he shot many wild things, among them a moose. He pissed on it (this doesn't sound bad in Nanai!) and then went on. He cut off a good piece and spoiled the rest.

He came home with a good take, bringing the best, the tastiest.

Later the other man woke up and went out hunting. He came to the meat the skull-man had left and looked it over. It looked good. He gathered it up and took it home. He gave it to his wife.

They set up a feast. The father wanted to taste and see who brought the best food. First he tasted the food the older sister had prepared.

"Foo, what is this nasty stuff?" he said. "I never ate such awful food." He was unhappy.

He went on to his younger daughter, and there the smells were wonderful. She put the food out on gold and silver plates. The floor was shining, the house was so beautiful, covered with something beautiful. On the table there was all kinds of food. He ate and said, "Never in my life have I tasted anything so delicious. Now if the man would only appear before my eyes I would be completely happy."

And so the man appeared to him for the first time, and they embraced. The young man bowed to him as a young man should before an older. The older man kissed the younger.

"Now I see that my daughter has found a real husband. I give my blessing for you to continue to live together."

That's the end of the story. ▼

Nadia noticed similarities between several of Lyubov's stories and personal names in Kondon and the stories and names of the Udegei who live in the Primorye territory to the south. It could be that trade relationships in the past led to an exchange.

This next story, however, is told all over the North and also in North America. It has the same flavour as the fox and bear relationship in the tale of Lakicho. The very end is like another tale told by the Evenk of Sakhalin, but with seals instead of the sheat-fish. Anna Khodzher tells a version with sea-worms (Khodzher 1998). Perhaps all the animal stories are connected on some level, in the same way that all the stories about Yegdyga and Belye, or Mergen and Pudi, seem to be part of one big network. The stories cannot be placed in a line but work in a spiral, each one picking up a part of the last and moving to a different place, a different possible outcome.

BEAR AND FOX

There once lived a bear. One time he was out walking and he saw a fox, with her tail in a crack in the ice.

"Fox, what are you doing?" he asked.

"What do you mean, what am I doing? Of course I'm

catching fish with my tail!"

"Ooh, that's interesting!" said the bear. "How do you do that?"

"Just like this. I put my tail down through the crack and catch them."

"I want to catch fish too," said the bear.

"Just sit down here and put your tail in the crack. I'll sit here next to you. We'll pull the fish out."

So the bear sat down and let his tail down into the crack. He sat and sat but nobody was taking hold of his tail.

"Fox!" he called out.

"*Ola?* Had enough?" said the fox. "No, you don't have any fish yet."

The bear sat there longer. He got tired of sitting. "Enough!" he called.

"No, you don't have any fish yet," said the fox. "Keep sitting, any minute now something will bite."

The bear sat and while he was there the ice froze strongly. He dozed off, and the next time he looked it was already morning. He looked around and that fox was nowhere to be seen. He wanted to get up and couldn't. He tried to pull his tail out. He pulled and pulled and couldn't get it out.

People came out, saw the bear and started to yell at him. "You're so bad," they called. They came after him and with one last pull he got free of the ice.

But he left part of his tail there, and that's why ever since then the bear has a short tail.

After that the bear ran along thinking, "Fox, I'm going to catch you. I don't know what I'll do when I get you but I will catch you."

And then he went into one house and saw the fox lying there with closed eyes.

"Aha, fox, gotcha!"

"Don't bother me, don't bother me," said the fox.

"What are you doing?"

"I was lying here with my eyes closed tight with pitch and I was having such a wonderful dream! Don't bother me."

"Tell me your dream," said the bear.

"No I won't. You lie down yourself and maybe you too will have such a dream."

The bear lay down.

"Now, so that your dream will be even better, so your eyes close better, I'll smear them with pitch."

"Oh yes, rub it on," said the bear.

"Lie down and close your eyes tight."

The bear lay down and the fox rubbed his eyes with pitch and then ran away.

The bear slept awhile and didn't dream anything. And when he wanted to open his eyes they didn't open! He couldn't see a thing. He tried and tried and couldn't open his eyes. Finally he got some little cracks open and thus his eyes have stayed narrow ever since.

"Fox, you tricked me again," he thought, "I'm going to find you and teach you a lesson." He walked off and soon he saw the fox sledding.

"Fox, I've got you!" he called.

"Not me. That's probably another fox you're looking for," said the fox.

"Oh, I guess the one I was looking for ran away. What are you doing here?"

"Me? Oh, I'm sledding."

"How wonderful. I want to try."

"Sit down on the sled. Just go up this little hill and then come down – it's great!"

The bear got on the sled and the fox gave him such a push! He flew down the hill and crashed to his death.

The fox had many more adventures. At last she wound up on an island, carried there by a bird, I think. The fox was stuck there on that island and started to sing a song, crying.

A sheat-fish came up to the surface. "Why are you crying?" he asked.

"I'm not crying," answered the fox. "I'm singing!" And then she asked, "How many relatives do you have?"

"I have many," answered the fish.

"Let's count them. I think I have more relatives than you."

"No," said the fish, "I have more."

"Call them all up to the surface and I'll count them."

So the fish called all his relatives and they came to the surface. They filled the whole water. And the fox started to count in Nanai, it's a sort of counting rhyme, "amun dyur elandu." It sounds funny. And as she counted she jumped from fish to fish and got all the way across to the other shore with dry feet. And the last fish – she broke his belly!

That's the way she repaid kindness. And that's the way she tricked those fish. And then she played tricks on some-one else too![4] ▼

There is a hill opposite Kondon that people say is a sleep-ing dragon. He has slept there for a long time, protecting the people of the village. His heart is visible on the other side of the river. It wasn't easy to find someone with a motor boat to take us for a ride to see the rest of the dragon, because the day we wanted to go happened to be the open-ing of the hunting season. But at last we found a man who had not succeeded in getting a hunting permit in time.

It was a long way to find the dragon's head, but at last there it was – you can see his teeth in the rocky cliffs. Then we went back several kilometres the other way, passing the small hills that form the dragon's body until we got to the tail, where it flows into the ground. Near the end of the tail there is a very clean spring right beside the river. People pass-ing by in boats stop there to wash and take a drink, paying their respects to the spirit of the spring. The water was deli-cious, and I enjoyed the feeling of being close to that most powerful of Nanai deities, the dragon master of the sky.[5]

When we got back, Lyubov introduced us to Ksenia

Digor, one of the elders of the village, known for her storytelling. She was born in 1915. We sat with her on her enclosed porch, away from most of the mosquitoes, while the sounds of house-building and motor repair resounded around us. Unlike many tellers who face the translator, she spoke her tale in Nanai and addressed it directly to me as if I understood. Even without knowing the language, it seemed to me that this tale would also be funny. Later that evening Lyubov listened to my tape and translated it. But she took issue with the telling and added another part of the story herself.[6]

GIRL-BRIDE AND FROG-BRIDE

There lived an old man who had two sons. One time both sons got married. One found himself a normal girl and the other one married a frog. In fact that happened at the end of another story. Why didn't grandmother tell you that one?

Anyway, they married and lived. After a while the old man thought, "I'll go and see how my older son's wife cooks." He went to her and said, "Cook me something so I can try it and see how you do." She quickly cooked him some food and served it to him. He was well satisfied.

He sat there and smoked his pipe. Then he said, "Now I want to warm myself by the fire." She went out and appealed to her brothers in the sky. They helped her to gather branches and she started the fire in the hearth. The old man sat happily warming himself. He lay there a while and finally said, "Fine, I've eaten well, rested well. You've done well."

He went home, and stayed there for a while. Then he thought, "Now I'll go and see the wife of my younger son." That's the one who had a frog wife. Fine, he came to her and said, "Daughter, I want to see how you prepare food.

Nanai storyteller Ksenia Digor with her grandchildren, Kondon.

Make me something to eat." So she went to the swamp and gathered grasses together with frog blood and all those baby frogs. She too appealed to her frog brothers who helped her. She brought the whole thing back, cooked it up and placed it before him. He took a bite and spit it right out! "What are you doing giving me this inedible food?"

He sat there a while longer and then said, "I'm feeling cold. Prepare the hearth for me quickly." She went out and gathered a lot of wet branches. She started the fire and it smoked terribly. The old man sat there and coughed. Tears poured from his eyes. He waved his arms and ran away.

And that's the end of that story. ▼

Lyubov says the story begins like this.

There was a girl who lived with her seven brothers. They lived for some time and then she got the feeling that some unclean power was coming. She quickly sent those seven brothers up into the heavens. She set out food for the *burkhans*, the *sevéns* that people used to feed. She put it out wherever possible, in every corner, and then she waited.

She turned herself into a hundred needles and hid behind the house-pole and waited. Pretty soon along came that unclean power, called *apa* in Nanai. He said, "Where has that Pudi gone?" She kept quiet there behind the pole.

But one little *sevén* spoke up, one she had forgotten about, and said, "She gave food to everyone and forgot me. I'll tell everything." And he informed about everything she had done.

"I've got you now!" said the evil spirit. He reached into the nets behind the pole, picked up those hundred needles, and took them away.

Then an old woman protector appeared. *Apa* had forgotten one needle and the old woman came and got it after he left. She turned that one needle back into the girl and ran away with her so that he wouldn't find her.

She had a thing to ride on that dug in the ground as it moved ahead. Behind them a broom swept away the tracks. She set the girl up on that thing and then disappeared. The girl went on, riding this thing that was digging ahead and sweeping away the tracks behind. She rode on and finally jumped off onto a hump in the swamp.

Out jumped a frog. It turned out to be her house the girl had landed on. The frog called out to the girl, "What are you doing destroying my home?"

The girl said, "I'll help you to rebuild it if you will take me to live with you." And so she lived there. She turned herself into a little stick. The grandmother turned her into a little stick. And the stick could walk. Sometimes she turned into a girl and sometimes she was that stick.

They lived together and then along came these two brothers, sons of that old man in the other part of the story. As usual, the older brother wasn't quite all there and the younger was smarter. The older one asked, "*khure* (frog), why do you have two *tapchan*, two beds?"

"Oh, I have two *tapchan* because, well, I embroider on the good one and on the bad one I sleep."[7]

And the younger brother didn't ask anything but lay down on that empty bed. They spent the night. While he was sleeping the younger brother found that stick and chipped it with his knife. Blood came out. He took the stick and hid it. He didn't tell anyone.

So the next day when they got ready to leave, the older brother offered his hand to the frog, and she agreed gladly. They got married and all went home together.

They arrived at the old man's settlement and the older brother said, "I have married this frog."

The younger brother didn't say anything like that and thus they started to live.

One day when he came home, he threw the stick over his left shoulder and it turned into a girl. And her finger had a cut on it where he had cut the stick with his knife. It was bandaged up just as he had wrapped the stick after he cut it.

And so he married her. And that's how the two brothers got married, one to a girl and the other to a frog. And further the story goes the way grandmother told it. ▼

The fact that the girl's essence was contained in the hundred needles and also in one single needle is reminiscent of the passing of shamanic power through the finger in the story of the Passar shaman,[8] and of the fact that our DNA repeats itself in every cell.

The second story Ksenia told took on some of Lyubov's laughter in the translation. The girl's warning to the old women not to do up their ties is reminiscent of a Nanai pregnancy taboo. It is thought that tying articles of clothing can make for a difficult birth. The rich old woman also shows an unwillingness to let things go, which means she does not contribute to the cycle of exchange that the Nanai value.

TWO OLD WOMEN AND THEIR PANTS

There once lived one poor old woman and one rich old woman. That poor old woman had only one pair of fish-skin pants. One day she went to the river to wash them. She washed and washed and then suddenly they washed away with the current.

She ran along the bank after them calling, "Oh, my one and only pair of pants, sewn from fish-skin, where are you going?" She ran and ran, thinking, how will I live without them?

She ran a long way down the river and then came to a house. Out from the house came a girl.

"Grandmother, why are you crying?" she asked.

"My only pair of pants has gone down the river. How will I live without them?"

"Don't worry, I'll give you new pants. I'll give you silk ones."

"No, I don't need anything like that. I need my own."

"Well, don't worry, come to my place. I'll give you something."

"All right," the old woman agreed.

Then the girl asked, "Which staircase do you want to go up; the golden, the silver, or the clay?"

"I'm just a poor old woman. I can go by the clay steps."

And so the girl took her up the clay stairs.

And then she asked her, "Grandmother, grandmother, which house would you rather enter; the golden, the silver, or the clay?"

"I'm a poor old woman, I'm not used to wealth. I'd better go into the clay house." And so the girl took her into the clay house.

Then she said, "Grandmother, grandmother, which pipe shall I give you to smoke, this long gold one brought from China, this slightly shorter silver one or this simple clay pipe?"

"I'm just a poor old woman, I'm not used to this wealth, better give me the clay pipe."

So the girl gave her the clay pipe and asked, "Grandmother, grandmother, what kind of tobacco shall I give you to smoke in the pipe, tobacco brought from China, that which was grown here, or shall I give you the tobacco that the cat shit?" (For some reason that sounds all right in Nanai but in Russian it comes out bad!)

"I'm just a poor old woman, I can smoke that last one, give it to me." And so the girl gave it to her, and the old woman smoked.

While she was serving the old woman, the girl brought out a box, and said, "Grandmother, I'm going to give you this box. Take it with you. Just make sure to be careful as you go along the road. If your shoe-laces come undone, don't do them up. If your belt comes undone, also don't do it up. And the same with your scarf, don't tie it up. Go home that way. When you get home, lie down to sleep. And when you wake up, don't be afraid of anything."

The girl saw her off and the old woman started home. On the way home her scarf came undone and she left it there along the way. Her belt came undone and the belt stayed there along the way. She went further and the ties on her shoes came undone. She didn't even look but just kept going.

When she arrived home, she put the box down and lay

down to sleep. During the night she woke up. She opened her eyes and thought, "My goodness, why is it so light in the house? It's as if the sun were shining. That's strange."

She went outside and saw the stars and the moon shining. And in the house everything was shining golden. There was wealthy clothing. Everything was rich there, dishes, all kinds of food. So in the end, the girl had rewarded the old woman.

In the morning the old woman got up. That day the wealthy old woman came to visit her.

"Where did you get such wealth?" she asked.

And the old woman told her everything. How she went down to the river to wash her pants. How they washed away.

The rich old woman thought, "How am I worse than that other woman? I also want gold things, rich silk dresses." And she took her silk pants and went down to the river to wash them. She let them go, and then ran along the shore crying, "Oh my silk pants, my only pants, where have you gone?"

She ran and ran and arrived at that place where that girl lived. The girl took her by the hand and asked, "Grandmother, grandmother, why are you crying?"

"How can I not cry? My silk pants have washed away. How can I live without them, my favourites?"

"Don't cry, I will give you something if you wish."

"All right," said the old woman.

The girl took her home.

"What road will you go by; the golden, the silver, or the clay?"

And the old woman answered, "Of course I'm not a poor old woman, of course I'll go by the golden." And the girl took her up the golden road.

They went up. There were three houses there, and the girl asked, "Grandmother, which house will you enter, the golden, the silver, or the clay?"

"I'll go into the golden. What do you think I am,

poverty-stricken?" And the girl took her in and seated her at the table. She asked, "Grandmother, which pipe will I give you; the one from China, the silver or the clay one?"

"Well, of course I will take the one from China." So the girl gave her the gold pipe and then asked, "Grandmother, which kind of tobacco will I use to fill the pipe?"

"Of course I want the best tobacco from China. I don't need that cat shit." So the girl silently filled the pipe and afterwards went to see old woman off and gave her a birchbark container.

"Grandmother, as you go along the road, if any of your things that are tied come undone, don't do them up and don't look in the box."

"All right, I'll do as you say, just give me my box and I'll go." And so she set out.

As she walked along, her scarf came undone. She thought, "Why should I lose my scarf?" and she did it up. Her belt came undone and she did it up. She walked further and her boot ties also came undone and she did them up.

She got home and set the container down right in the middle of the house and said to her old man, "Let's lie down to sleep."

In the night she woke up. It was dark in the house. She didn't understand. She went outside and it was daylight.

"What's going on here?" she thought. In the house there was dirt. They opened the box there were snakes and all kind of filth. The snakes bit them and they died.

And that's how the story ends. The poor old woman opened the box and there was all kinds of gold and wealth. ▼

The trip was nearing an end. Nadia and I made one more short voyage out from Khabarovsk; this time to the city of Amursk and the nearby Nanai village of Achan.

In Amursk we made our way through the still-rainy streets to visit Maria Borisovna Kile, widow of Pongsa Kon-

Nanai shaman Nyura Kile with her husband, Bolon.

stantinovich, who was a well-known Nanai cultural activist. His writing and organizational activities did much to preserve Nanai culture during a difficult time and Maria Borisovna keeps his memory alive and promotes his work.

She told us that the Nanai language expresses all the beauty of nature. The Nanai have a very visual memory, and the language contains a lot of detail in describing nature. This is why it is difficult to translate the stories. Conversation turned to the fact that the Nanai language has its own words for southern creatures such as crocodiles, monkeys, and elephants. Why would this be, asks Maria Borisovna, if the people had never seen those animals? This reminded us of our conversation with Valentina Kyalundzyuga on the same subject, where she described crocodiles in the rivers and told a tale of monkeys.⁹ It reminded Maria Borisovna of this legend.

THE CROCODILE

A man had a daughter. They went out to a lake and the man made many things of birch-bark: containers, even a house. Then he went off to hunt and his daughter stayed alone.

When he came back she was gone. He immediately had a bad feeling that something was wrong and went to look for her. He started throwing the birchbark containers into the lake and it was as if something were swallowing them.

Then he saw something large and dead, belly-up in the lake. He pulled it out and it was a crocodile. He quickly cut it open to find what was left of his daughter. In the belly of the crocodile he found her ring, nothing more. The bark things had also disappeared.

I think the girl probably dangled her legs in the water or maybe just didn't notice the crocodile sunning himself on the rocks. ▼

In Achan we stayed with Nina Pavlovna Khodzher, who ran a very active children's ensemble. Nina said she had been invited to accompany the shamans to America in 1994 but had decided against it. She believes it is dangerous for her people to risk the health of their elders and that it would have been just as useful for Americans to listen to people who know about shamanism, instead of the shamans themselves.

She took us to see shaman Nyura Sergeevna Kile, who was born in 1907 in the neighbouring village of Bolon.

Nanai embroidery artist Vera Grigorievna Khodzher, Achan.

Nina Pavlovna consults her to learn what things can be shown in the ensemble and what should not be, as well as the ways of carrying out rituals.

Nyura first showed us how she cuts designs from fishskin, which are later covered with embroidery. I am often hesitant about taking photos, especially with shamans. This time I was just getting ready to ask her permission when Nyura turned to Nina and said in a loud stagewhisper, "Aren't there going to be any photographs?"

Then she spoke about being a shaman. "I am just a little shaman," she said, meaning that she does not accompany the dead. "You must not sing shamanic songs in the spring, because at that time the spirits are flying and you might get sick." The *Kasa* ceremony is necessary, she thought – but it can't be done by a shaman from elsewhere. Nadia had been thinking of inviting a shaman from central Siberia, where shamanic revival was already strong and many hereditary shamans were practicing, as such a person might be able to help with the problems of the Amur region. But Nyura said that it must be a local person.

She agreed to put on her belt, take up the drum, and show us how she dances. This was not a real ceremony, of course, and she had to hold a special conversation, called *ypila*, with her spirits, asking forgiveness for doing things in a way that was not completely correct. I think this may be why the shamans who visited the United States often asked forgiveness, of both their own spirits and the local ones.

She took her *sevéns* and *yampa* from under the bed. They were carefully wrapped up. Then she fed the *sevéns* with vodka. She had us all put on the belt, one by one, take up the drum, and dance. This time I was glad I already knew that I was supposed to make the shaman laugh. And she did! Then she danced. As with Adikhini in Gvasyugi, I was amazed at how graceful these elderly women are – it is indeed a gift. She prayed for good health for all people.

My last meeting of 1995 was with Maria Antonovna Beldi, who is a *tudin*. In Nanai tradition the *tudin* is neither a

shaman nor an assistant, has no costume or drum, and is
not consecrated. Some of them can do healings but mainly
they diagnose illness by meditating to see causes. They can
determine what *sevén* figures should be made. Some say that
they were more trusted than shamans. They can follow the
shaman on the journey and occasionally keep the shaman
from going astray in another world. Anna Smolyak cites one
instance when a *tudin* prevented a shaman from returning
the wrong soul to a woman's body! The *tudin* and storyteller
can both see some of what the shaman sees and can report
on his/her activities (Smolyak 1991, 46–9).

Maria Antonovna is highly respected and frequently
called on by her own people to answer questions relating to
shamanism and culture. "To call kya-kya asks forgiveness of
the spirits," she said. She had picked the ability up from
hearing it done in her childhood.[10]

Maria Antonovna came to Achan in 1948, when she got
married. She had heart trouble during her first pregnancy.
"One grandmother came to visit me all the time. 'Let's
make a *sevén*,' she said. She made it of wood, or ordered it
from a craftsman. It had the shape of a heart with dogs on
both sides. The grandmother started to chant, and burned
the ledum plant beside a cup of water. But my heart didn't
get much better.

"The old woman came often. 'You know this *sevén* is acting on me, influencing me. As I begin kya-kya I feel pulled,
called to heaven,' she said. And then I started to feel better.
It's essential to have the smell of ledum – if there was no way
to burn it, they put it in water. This old woman was not a
shaman, but an ordinary person who could help. Not everyone could do it, but some could."

Maria Antonovna said her grandmother was a good shaman. Her name was Khaosaka, meaning paper. "She was as
white and as light as paper. Her spirits went through the
water and air. She turned into a turtle and into lizards.
Those were her helper spirits, and she called them all. Spirits take the form they need to solve problems," said Maria

Antonovna. While this seems to differ from other versions where spirits have specialties and the shaman calls the appropriate one in each given case, it may simply be a different expression of the same spiritual concept.

Maria also recalled a healing done to get rid of *amban*. "The people made a man of hay and hung him opposite the window. The shaman invited three men to hold it. She began to shamanize and the hay man jumped around. Finally it lay still. Then they burnt it or threw it out. The evil spirit had been removed from the sick person.

"In one year a shaman healed many people and then in the fall all those who had been healed came to her to give her strength. At that time they all beat the drum."

A number of people had gathered that day to listen to Maria Antonovna and ask her questions about the importance of *Kasa*. Several shamans had said that the reason society is plagued with so much drunkenness is that there are many souls hanging around the villages who have not been seen off to the next world. Nyura Kile believes there is one woman who could do it, but for some reason the woman is unwilling. Maria Antonovna said that some shamans have been known to conduct the dead without actually being *Kasa* shamans. Others consider it dangerous to try without being fully qualified.

They all agreed that these unescorted souls were causing problems for the living. Souls that are not sent off properly turn into evil spirits. The men were suffering more severely than the women. Why the men suffered more was not explained, but it was mentioned that more of them have died "not their own death" – in wars, fighting, or through suicide. More of their souls have been left unaccompanied. Indigenous men suffer from the fact that their traditional way of life has been disrupted by collectivization and the repression of typically male sports and shamanic activities, while women's lives have been less disrupted. They remain at the centre of the home, where they have always been, energized by responsibility and their folk traditions of embroidery and storytelling.

Is *Kasa* a grieving or a holiday? "It's like a holiday," one woman said. "It cannot be closed or forbidden to outsiders, as some would like. Now the old women say among themselves that spirits are walking among us. They complain that they themselves have just been thrown away as not needed. Nobody listens to them."

Maria had seen a *Kasa* ceremony done in the village of Jari. A special *Kasa* shaman had to come from elsewhere to send the soul to *Buni*.[11] At the *Kasa* they made big wood spirit figures, called *dyuli*, and dressed them. Then the shaman did the ritual. She asked the *dyuli* if the spirit of the dead person agreed to go. Once one of them said no. Why? His wife had slept with another man before the end of three years. "I need blood," said the spirit of the dead husband. They hit the woman hard and spread her blood on the wooden *dyuli*. Then the dead man was satisfied and agreed to go. The shaman accompanied the soul to the next world and saw to it that he was established there before coming back.[12]

It is still not clear who will take over the important role of escorting the dead. Younger generations remember the power of older shamans – what they did, what they told about. But so far few young people have shown an awareness of being chosen by the spirits. Nadia tells of a young Udegei woman who dreamed that an old white-haired Udegei man spoke to her, saying that the ceremony of accompanying the dead must be conducted. He used words that the young woman did not know, but she remembered them and Valentina Kyalundzyuga confirmed that they were the Udegei name for the ceremony, *Khanyaunya khuni*. Perhaps this is a beginning.

After Achan I went back to Khabarovsk and from there to Canada. Over the years the process of reentry into my own culture has become both simpler and more complex. After my early trips to Sakhalin and Chukotka I would return home to stand transfixed in the produce section of our

The first day of school, September 1995, Achan.

small co-op store, stunned by the quantity and quality of what we can eat, in or out of season. At the same time I was relieved to be speaking my own language, washing clothes in a machine, preparing my own food – I was glad just to be home. But now I've become more comfortable in the Khabarovsk Territory, well cared for not only because I'm a guest but as part of a network that takes care of people on general principles. Friends from Khabarovsk Territory have now sat at my kitchen table in Canada, and this too shifts the balance.

But communicating what I have learned is not much easier than it was at first. Many North Americans still believe that indigenous people in Siberia have been untouched by the events of the communist years, perhaps wanting to believe that there is still a place on earth that is uncorrupted by the twentieth century.

What is the connection between our traditions and our contemporary lives? What strengths do we take from the beliefs of our ancestors, even if we were raised in a very different context than they were? For me, trying to answer these questions is where acquaintance with a new culture becomes personal. Friends who started as "informants" and working colleagues have become friends of the kitchen table, engaged in the same quest for understanding.

When I return to North America I try to build a bridge between two places and their worldviews. People on this side of the ocean tend to assume that people on the other side are more spiritually developed or oriented than we are, as if we could turn to them for answers. This may be true, but it is not the whole story. To them the idea seems ridiculous. Even if they are more spiritually oriented, we can't forget that they are obsessed with daily life, buying food, going to work, dealing with children. While it is true that being in Russia is a profound spiritual experience for me, I have the sense that this is because of my quest rather than a reflection of their daily lives. They, on the other hand, think that they can turn to me for answers about the market economy, as if all North Americans were experts in business. I now think that defining people as more spiritual or as business experts is part of creating distance, of making them seem exotic.

Can we equate the concept "more spiritual" with "less materialistic?" People who have very few material goods available cannot be materialistic in the same way – they are not constantly distracted by the technology, by the complexity, of consumer culture. But remaking the spiritual link with nature is just as much of a challenge in that culture as it is in my own.

The contact with nature essential to shamanic philosophy was held up to ridicule by communist ideology and physically broken by the move away from the traditional relationship to the land. This connection is one of the themes that runs through the stories I heard, and through discussions for the future. Another theme is protection from danger, which is of tremendous importance in facing today's unknowns. It is no accident that so many of the stories told include animal transformations, as well as death and rebirth. As the social order and its external values change, people work to retain the essentials of their culture, just as an individual's basic character stays the same no matter how we change our external appearance and way of life. Contacts are being deliberately maintained with ancestors and between past and present, humans and nature. Networks connect people up and down the Amur.

Stories told today relate to today's problems - the invention of the Nanai violin is a model for the revival of culture while embroidery has taken on a new protective value by providing economic development. Values that encourage the practice of mutual aid are essential in a time of transformation.

Women are taking leadership roles in their communities, creating employment schemes, advising, educating. I saw them finding new forms for their embroidery work, new markets in which to raise money to support their families. They manage homes alone as their men lose jobs and became unreliable. I see in these activities a reflection of the girls who lived alone, who created new life from disaster, who survived hard times and ingeniously outwitted the powers of evil.

The spirits may or may not call new shamans in the coming time, and young people may or may not respond if they do. But at least some people are open to the possibility of new shamans appearing. People already call on Dr Lyuba Passar and other medical doctors who use some shamanic methods for healing and advice, as if they were shamans.

It is almost certain that the traditional languages will not survive long into the twenty-first century in everyday speech. But one certainty is that the storytelling process continues, around kitchen tables, in offices and gardens. Elements of tradition run through the new stories. Women's minds are at work on the question of healing their men and raising their children to a responsible, possible life. As we were leaving, shaman Nyura Kile said, "Without a dream, how can a thing happen?" I'm sure I'll be back in the Amur region again and again, visiting with friends, listening to stories, watching and participating in change, seeing dreams become reality.

Appendix One:
History of the Amur Peoples

The history of settlement in the region of the lower Amur
River and the Primorye Territory goes back at least 30,000
years. Stone tools and other evidence of settlement have
been found at Suchu Island, Nizhnye Khalby, and other
archaeological sites. Beginning with the neolithic (fourth
to second millennia BC) there is a continuity of artistic style
from ancient pottery motifs and petroglyphs to contemporary embroidery and carving designs (Okladnikov 1981, 7).

Some of the most striking examples of early art in the
Amur area are the petroglyphs at Sikachi Alyan. They are
extremely well-preserved and show masterful representations of spiral motifs, land and water birds, and animals
such as moose, bear, and tiger. The sun and moon and even
shaman's masks appear engraved in rock along the river
bank. Whether or not these motifs were interpreted then as
they are today, their appearance shows the antiquity of the

spiritual concepts that underly the shamans' stories. Many of the same motifs also appear embroidered on contemporary clothing.

Although today the climate is temperate, with cold winters and heavy snows, there is some evidence that in early times the area was much warmer – even today the Udegei and Nanai tell ancient tales of crocodiles and monkeys and have names for these animals in their own languages. Amur cultures may have been more connected with those to the south in early times. According to Nanai historian V.I. Geiker, the Nivkh language has some words in common with the languages of the Philippines, although I have not heard this anywhere else. The petroglyph designs, as well as the patterns used for the tattoos of the women in Chukotka, may also be connected to more southern cultures.

At the end of the neolithic, around 1000 BC, the ancestors of today's Tungus-language peoples began to move into what are now the Khabarovsk and Primorye Territories. They came from the area around Lake Baikal and as far south as Mongolia, driven from their ancient homeland by the incursion of Turkic and Mongolian peoples who were part of the huge movements going on throughout the Central Asian steppeland at the time, and which continued through the time of Chinghis Khan and beyond.

Some of the Turks and Mongols (ancestors of today's Tuvan and Buriats, among others) intermarried with some of the Tungus people who had stayed in Central Asia while others moved eastward.[1] The northern Tungus peoples spread out tremendously – there are now Even and Evenk people all the way from Buriatia on the banks of Baikal northeast into Chukotka and southeast into the northern part of the Khabarovsk Territory. The southern Tungus and Manchu people (Nanai, Udegei, Ul'chi, Negidal, Solon) now live in the south of Khabarovsk Territory, in the Primorye Territory, and in China. The Nanai and Ul'chi people live at the meeting place of north and south and their clans trace their heritage in both directions – the Khodzher,

Beldi, Geiker and Passar clans to the Manchu and the Samar and Digor to the Evenk.

When the Tungus peoples arrived in the far east, they met the ancestors of today's Ainu and Nivkh, who had already been there for thousands of years. Some southern Tungus intermarried with them, while others retained their own separate identities.

These ancestors of the Ainu and Nivkh had been in the lower Amur much longer than the newcomers – several thousand years at least. Their languages are both isolates although they have many words in common with languages of the Altai families, presumably borrowed through contact. Their cultures have much in common with those of Chukotka and Kamchatka, as well as with those of their Tungus neighbours. Today the Nivkh live on northern Sakhalin Island and at the mouth of the Amur, while most Ainu live on Hokkaido in Japan.

The complex population movements and wars of the Middle Ages have affected the history of the Amur area and even of China and Europe. Mongolian and Manchurian cultures and governments developed near this region and swept across whole continents.

In the seventh to tenth centuries the Bokhai government flourished, as did the government that followed it, that of the Jurchen-udegei, direct ancestors of the Manchus who ruled all of China for almost 300 years (1644–1911) and of several of the Amur peoples. In the eleventh to thirteenth centuries the Jurchen established themselves in a series of well-fortified cities in present-day Primorye Territory, Manchuria, and North Korea and grew wealthy through trading valuable furs for goods from China. They lived in towns but grew crops and kept domestic animals. As trade developed further and furs became the main medium of exchange, pottery and metal-working skills were lost among the Amur peoples.

Written Chinese records describe the Jurchen as fierce fighting people – even the name carries the meaning "stub-

born, fighters." Some of the northern tribes were independent of the Jurchen Golden Empire, while others were
included in it. Among the more independent tribes were
some of the people known as Udige, or "wild" people, a term
that at that time was probably applied to several northern
tribes, not only to those known today as the Udegei.

In the first half of the twelfth century, Mongols, under
the leadership of Khamar Mongol, attempted to establish
themselves in the area, building several forts. In 1161 they
were defeated by the Jurchen and fell into warring factions.
It was not until 1206 that all the Mongols were united
under Temujin, or Chinghis-khan. In 1210 he declared war
on the Jurchen and in the 1230s burned the cities of the
Primorye and took over the area (Shavkunov 1990, 50).

The Udige tribes resisted the Mongols and were largely
destroyed by them. Some managed to flee to the inaccessi-
ble forests rather than give in to the invaders. There they
began to live by nomadic hunting and gathering, giving up
their permanent homes, crops, and livestock. Although
some later settled in fishing villages along the Amur, others
remained nomadic through seven centuries until the Soviet government forced them to settle in the permanent villages where they live today.

The more westerly Jurchen people, ancestors of today's
Manchurians, gave in to the Mongols without a struggle
and were allowed a great degree of cultural and political
autonomy. They were able to maintain their way of life
almost unchanged and after the fall of the Mongol Yüan
dynasty (1644) ruled all of China. There are still close connections in language and culture between the peoples of
Manchuria and of the lower Amur.

For at least a thousand years there has been constant
contact between the peoples of the Amur and their Turkic,
Mongolian, and Manchu neighbours. Separated by huge distances, they remain close in terms of religious beliefs and
oral traditions. Mythic image is connected by a long history.

In the sixteenth century Russians began to arrive in the

Amur region, looking for furs and for access to the Pacific Ocean. In the nineteenth century their influence became very powerful, not only in terms of the fur trade but through direct political control and missionary activity. Their relations with indigenous people became more and more oppressive, and included heavy taxation. Political pressure from China following disputes over territory also contributed to stronger control. The railroad, completed in the 1890s, brought many Russian and Ukrainian settlers to the region. Their activities were mainly agricultural at first and did not compete directly with the indigenous peoples except inasmuch as ploughing and clearing land reduced animal habitat. Later the settlers began to trade in furs and competition became more direct. The rivers were fished out, the people impoverished. Nanai historian Valery Khodzher says that "The idea that Russia took over peacefully is a myth – there was war between the Ul'chi and the Cossacks. Russians sent people dying of typhus and smallpox down the river on rafts in order to spread those diseases."[2]

Most peoples of the Amur did not adopt Christianity but retained their own beliefs, sometimes adding the "Russian God" to their pantheon, since he was seen as powerful. But he never completely replaced the time-honoured local deities and people were baptised more from political expediency than from belief.

What was traditional life like for women of the Amur region? As usual in hunting/gathering and fishing societies, labour was divided on gender lines, with men going out to hunt and fish and women remaining close to the home, gathering plants and preparing food and clothing.

Among all the Amur peoples, it was forbidden to marry within one's own clan. After marriage women moved to the homes of their husbands, sometimes far from their own families. A new wife was under the authority of her husband's mother, and how her life went after marriage depended on her husband's success and on how well she got along with her new family. Clan structure was especially complex among the Nivkh. Both men and women had some degree of sexual freedom within the limits of the structure, although Bruce Grant's interviews with Nivkh women in the mid-1990s show that this freedom was much more rarely practiced than nineteenth-century Russian ethnographers believed (Shternberg 1999, 214).

In earlier times it was not unusual for a Nanai, Ul'chi, or Udegei man to have more than one wife, but women had only one husband. Udegei Valentina Kyalundzyuga tells of her mother coming to her husband's family as a second wife when she was only five. The little girl grew up calling the first wife "mama." Later the Soviet government made it illegal for a man to have more than one wife. In their case, the older wife had to leave the home. When the younger wife died of illness, the older one returned.

Because women moved to live with their husband's families after marriage, they contributed to the diffusion of knowledge and values on a different level than men, who met those outside their clan in trade situations.

Although the lives of women in these societies seem bleak in descriptions by early Soviets authors, there is some reason to believe that the situation was exaggerated in order to make Soviet innovations appear to be great improvements. Certainly many women held positions of respect and acted as heads of households when their husbands died or went away on long hunting and trading trips. As in other hunting and gathering societies, the men did most of the hunting and the women most of the gathering. Beyond this there was no great specialization of occupation. Hunting provided the most valued part of the diet and skins for clothing, but hunting takes place only sporadically and is not always reliable. Plant foods and fish provided by the women served as a more constant source of food, and the women's role in preserving food and making clothing was vital. In addition to their central role in the family, women were respected as shamans and as tellers of historic epics. In many cases, however, the lives of women were particularly difficult, with arranged marriages forcing girls to leave their own families and sometimes to live like slaves in their husbands' homes. The theme of abuse is common in tales told today.

With the revolution of 1917 and the subsequent incursion of Soviet power to the distant reaches of the Soviet Union, there were massive change to the Amur peoples' way of life. Although hunting and fishing continued, these activities were collectivized and people brought together to live in villages instead of nomadic camps. Eventually wages replaced the ancient systems of distribution. This new system encouraged individualism, while the old had led to mutual aid. The economy was now organized around the goal of taking as much as possible from the environment, while the hunting society had made a point of taking only what was needed. Collectives were organized not only for hunting and fishing but also for activities that were not traditional in the area, such as agriculture. Specialization of activity reduced the flexibility that had ensured survival in the past.

New houses were built, electricity installed, schools opened. Communications developed with other parts of the Soviet Union, at the same time as they were cut off with China. The Amur became more and more industrialized and the border with China was closely guarded. Indigenous people lost contact with their relatives across the border – contact re-established only in the 1990s.

In the early years, the cultural and educational policies of the Soviet Union encouraged certain aspects of indigenous language and culture. Marxist theory praised certain aspects of the "primitive communism" of native peoples. Alphabets were devised for previously unwritten languages (at first Latin-based and later Cyrillic), textbooks issued, folklore collected. At the same time traditional religious concepts were challenged in the move toward an atheistic society. In accordance with Marxist theory, people were urged to reject their "primitive" ways and to adopt new forms of dress, work, and marriage. Many children were educated in boarding schools, separated from their multi-generational families. Their own oral traditions were replaced with Russian folktales, and they learned the Russian language and skills for contemporary living. Children no longer learned all of their life skills from their families. As higher education became possible, many indigenous people trained as doctors and teachers. In the 1930s and 1940s policies became more stringent – the books that had been published in indigenous languages were burned and Russian became the common language.

Throughout the Soviet period the practice of shamanism was forbidden. Shamans were seen by the authorities as backward since many opposed the new regime. Often shamans received heavy prison sentences and died in the gulags. The policies were applied unevenly, however, and shamans continued to practice, especially in out-of-the-way villages with more sympathetic administrations.

With the disintegration of the Soviet Union, there has been new cultural and social freedom. But this is offset by massive economic and social problems. Collectives, with their workshops, have closed, people go months with no pay, medical facilities are overtaxed and underequipped, crime is on the rise. Vodka has become a medium of exchange, which exacerbates problems with alcoholism and violence.

These problems, which plague all parts of the former Soviet Union, are encouraging a return to self-reliance in the villages of the Amur. In summer people are very busy, growing gardens, fishing, and building and repairing houses, which are now privately owned. Part and parcel of this self-reliance is concern with the education of children so that they are prepared for contemporary professions as well as understanding their own ancient culture. So, in the midst of economic disaster, children's dance ensembles are thriving. Loss of language may be irreversible but the culture itself is flowering in the vacuum provided by political collapse. Today women play strong leadership roles in this area.

During the Soviet period, generations became increasingly separated. Children today do not speak the same language as their grandparents, since that older generation is the last to speak indigenous languages almost exclusively while children today speak Russian almost exclusively. Bridging that gap is one of the things today's leaders must deal with, but it must be done quickly because the older people are rapidly dying out. Shamans and storytellers are crucial to this process, both because their memories hold so much vital information and because they are the bridge to the spiritual basis of the culture.

Building decorated with Soviet art

Appendix Two:
Readings on Siberian
Shamanism

Much has been written about Siberian shamanism, from the descriptions of European and Oriental travelers and ethnographers like Lev Shternberg in the nineteenth century to the world wide web. There is a wealth of literature written in Russian and a growing body of work in English. Some of the most accessible works are Joan Halifax's *Shaman: The Wounded Healer* and Piers Vitebsky's *Shaman: An Illustrated Guide (Inner Wisdom)*, both of which contain beautiful photographs as well as excellent texts about shamanism in many areas of the world.

The best reference for shamanism in the Amur region specifically is the excellent work (in Russian only) of ethnographer Anna Smolyak, who details the world-view, life, costume, and rituals of Nanai and Ul'chi shamans. A painstakingly detailed historical work (in English, although difficult to read because of its archaic language) is

S.M. Shirokogoroff's *The Psychomental Complex of the Tungus*. The Tungus, now called Evenk, are related to the peoples of the Amur in language and culture.

One of the best general works on Siberian shamanism is *Izbranniki Dukhov* (Chosen of the Spirits) by Vladimir Basilov. Although this important work has not appeared in English, several of his articles appear in anthologies edited by Hoppál and others. Anna-Leena Siikala provides an important synthesis of works in various languages on shamanic rituals in *The Rite-Technique of the Siberian Shaman*. It would be difficult to talk about works on shamanism without mentioning Mircea Eliade's *Shamanism: An Archaic Technique of Ecstasy*, which most English-speakers rely on. Although Eliade did not do field-work in Siberia, his book contains a wealth of information gathered from other sources.

Caroline Humphrey has written extensively about shamanism among the Mongols and Buryats. In her more general article, "Theories of North Asian Shamanism," she outlines several of the debates current in the study of Siberian shamanism, and discusses the relevant literature. These debates include whether shamanism is a religion (as affirmed by most indigenous Siberians) or a technique (the view of many outsiders, following Eliade), and its historical roots. To this we can add questions of the shaman's sanity, no longer in doubt in the eyes of Western authors although still debated in Russia, and the question of whether today's shamanic activity represents a continuation of a long tradition or a revival after a true hiatus.

Less has been written about the role of storytelling in shamanism than about the shaman's rituals, artifacts, and mental state. Exceptions are the many works of Tuvan scholar Mongush Kenin-Lopsan on shamanic poetry and Elena Novik's *Obriad i fol'klor v sibirskom shamanisme (Rite and Folklore in Siberian Shamanism)*. Both of these author's work appear in translation in M. Balzer's *Shamanic Worlds: Rituals and Lore of Siberia and Central Asia*, which also contains important contributions from other scholars of Russia. A.T. Hatto has written about the connection between shamanism and epics. *The Tale of the Nisan Shamaness* (Nowak and Durant, with notes) is a marvelous epic tale of a Manchurian female shaman, taken from a culture which is directly related to those of the Amur. A Mongolian version of this story appears on the internet at www.geocities. com/Athens/Oracle/8226/nishan.html. Laurel Kendall (1987 and 1988) carefully examines the relationship between storytelling and the practice of female shamans in Korea.

There are a number of excellent collections in English of relevant articles by scholars from many countries, including works edited by Marjorie Balzer, Vilmos Dioszegi, Mihály Hoppál, and Shirley Nicholson.

The reader will find a large number of constantly changing websites devoted to shamanism. My current favorites are Shamanic Dimensions (www.shamanicdimensions.com), which contains a wealth of information on traditional and contemporary shamanism as well as information on workshops, research, and a complete bibliography; Where the Eagle Flies (www.siberianshamanism.com) which provides information about several present-day shamans and their activities in Europe; and the Foundation for Shamanic Studies (www.shamanism.org) with information about the foundation's experiential courses and other activities.

Notes

INTRODUCTION

1 I use the term "magic tale" instead of the more common "fairy tale" because I feel it better describes the product of a vision and carries fewer negative connotations in English.

2 For suggested readings on Siberian shamanism, see Appendix Two.

CHAPTER ONE

1 Now they are more often called "aborigeny" (aborigines) or "korennye zhiteli" (native dwellers).

2 Chikhya is an affectionate name, while Belye is a general term for a heroine.

3 *Sevén*: accent on the last syllable. Tungus language word for spirit figure. The word has no relation to the English "seven."

4 They are: г a soft g sound; ӈ a sound similar to ng in English "sing"; нь similar to n followed by y; and з, similar to j in English "joy".

5 *Kamlanie* is a Russian word which comes from the Turkic word for shaman, *kam*. It refers to shamans' ceremonials. For descriptions of shamans' ceremonies, including the use of laughter, see chapters 2, 6 and 8.

6 This story appears in Udegei and Russian, complete with the songs sung by Yegdyga and the seagull girls in Simonov 1998, 216–223.

7 In another version he goes in an iron boat.

8 Labrador tea is frequently used in ceremonies and as a disinfectant.

9 For more on Ul'chi and other bear ceremonies, see chapter 7.

10 See Evdokia Batovna Kimonko's "Brother and Sister," chapter 2.

11 See "Belye and Naundyaka," chapter 6.

12 See Shternberg 1999 for an extensive discussion of early marriage practices in the Amur region, particularly among the Nivkh.

13 And other animals. I have heard Amur tales of women marrying bears, tigers, snakes, crows, fish, and puppies – and even a skull and an old discarded hunting bag. Further to the north the indigenous Chukchi and Yupik people tell of women who marry whales and walrus. Valentina tells of a man who married a seal. All these tales reflect the intimate relationship between a hunting people and the animals who sustain their lives. "Biatu" is unusual among the bear stories in that it is the girl who initiates the marriage.

14 For more on sacred twins, see chapter 7.

15 This is similar to the custom of cutting the head of a shaman's drum when the shaman dies.

16 See "Gamuli" in chapter 6. The story appears in Udegei and Russian in Simonov 1998, 146–50.

17 She told this story again in 1998, based on her original transcriptions. In the newer version she named the human wife Kakta Ni, the half person, and described her as having golden hair, which may indicate that she was Russian. There was a

contest between the woman and the seal to see which was stronger and at last the seal managed to get away. As well, in the original version the man did not return to the sea at the end but continued to live in the new place with his seal-wife. A version similar to the 1998 one appears in Simonov 1998, 150–3. The editors note that the golden hair may show that this woman is a spirit being, perhaps daughter of the Master of the Sea. Turkic peoples have a female fire or sun deity with golden hair.

CHAPTER TWO

1 Many of the tales he collected are published in Russian in Simonov 1998.
2 There are also members of religious sects (Old Believers) living in central Siberia who never came under the Soviet government because nobody knew where they were. Some of these people have now emerged, unaware of events like World War II and even the Russian revolution.
3 This custom is well-known throughout the Central Asian parts of the Russian Federation as an offering to the spirits of mountain passes, sacred trees, and springs.
4 See "Biatu" in chapter 1.
5 The thought that he could have shot his sister in the form of a moose may have to do with the idea that a person can keep his/her soul outside the body. It is also possible that the moose is the sister's protector animal.
6 See Anna Khodzher's "The Puppy," Valentina Kyalundzyuga's "Palam Padu," and Lyubov Samar's "The Girl and the Skull."
7 This is a reasonable question, as people do sometimes see the souls of the dead.

CHAPTER THREE

1 For an excellent historical ethnography of the Nivkh, especially in the 20th century, see Grant 1995. Ethnography of the nineteenth century is best described in Shternberg 1999.

2 And eventually thousands, before the monetary system was reformed in 1999. The process is beginning again, however, as inflation is still not under control.

3 "Making up" is part of the process of story creation based on inner vision. Legends, on the other hand, can be verified by people other than the teller, since they report events that have happened in the world of ordinary reality. Shternberg writes that the best storytellers he encountered were improvising poets, usually shamans of the children of shamans, who would tell their tales while in trance. There were few with the stamina or patience to allow their lengthy epic poems to be recorded by hand so some of the most imaginative and visionary tales may have gone unrecorded. (Shternberg 1999, 10).

4 In general Russian policy in the tsarist period emphasized collecting tribute (*yasak*) from local people, but there were financial and political benefits for those who adopted Christianity and Russian names. Pimgun learned that story when she was little from Ivan Lopkanovïtch Pivrin, who died in 1980.

5 See chapter 6 for similar Ul'chi beliefs and customs.

6 The birds return to nest in the tree of life, from which the mother goddess sends them back to earth. The tree and birds are often represented on the back of a wedding dress.

7 In his work with the Chukchi in the late nineteenth century, Bogoras describes spontaneous sex-change among their shamans. Usually it was a man who turned into a woman. First the man changed his dress and social role and later there was sometimes a physical change as well (Bogoras 1975, 450–1). Shternberg, writing about the same time period, recalls several cases of hermaphrodites among the Nivkh of Sakhalin who were completely accepted in their communities. They were not shamans (Shternberg 1999, 130).

CHAPTER FOUR

1 The animals in these tales are often of indeterminate gender, as are Tungus pronouns, which do not distinguish between male and female.

2 See Anna Khodzher's "Frog, Mouse, and Moose," chapter 5.

3 "The Taimen Girl," chapter 7

4 See chapter 2, and the Ul'chi tale "Two Sisters" in chapter 6.

5 The Tuvans of south-central Siberia tell a similar story about the source of their bowed string instrument, the *igil*. In it, a boy mourns for his lost horse and makes the instrument using the horse's skin and hair.

6 Translated from Khodzher 1990, 56–61.

7 A verst is a measure of distance used in Tsarist times, equal to 1.06 km.

CHAPTER FIVE

1 See chapter 7 on shamans caring for children's souls.

2 See chapter 7 for descriptions by Anna Smolyak and Mado Dechuli of a similar place where shamans care for the souls of small children.

3 According to A. Smolyak, specialist in Nanai and Ul'chi shamanic traditions, there were three forms of Nanai shamans. The weakest, called *mepu-sama*, could heal only themselves. The second category, *taochini-sama*, could conduct healings and other ceremonies. The highest form of shamans, *kasaty-sama*, conducted the souls of the dead to the next world (Smolyak 1991, 51–3).

4 The Russian word *bioenergetika* is closer to the North American concept of magnetic or energy healing than it is to bioenergetics.

CHAPTER SIX

1 Although there is no strict policy dividing native villages from Russian, most are predominantly one or the other.

2 By 1998, Valentina tells me, tigers were coming right into people's gardens.

3 This is very similar to the way Valentina described her own father's funeral. See chapter 2.

4 See "Crocodile," chapter 8.

420

5 Accent on the last syllable. Another version of this story appears in Udegei and Russian in Simonov 1998, 260–5.

6 See chapter 8 "Girl Bride and Frog Bride."

7 This story appears in Udegei and Russian in Simonov 1998, 226–35. The editors explain that the squirrels took revenge on the brothers because one of them had cruelly wounded a squirrel.

8 "The Terrible Frog," chapter 4.

9 See discussion of marriage customs in chapter 1.

10 Similar to the version in Simonov 1998, 146–9.

11 Simonov (1998, 388) points out that among the Udegei wealth was respected and admired in folk tales, since is shows a person's ability.

CHAPTER SEVEN

1 This heating system is similar to that in rural Chinese houses.

2 Shternberg discusses the bear as a clan member (1999,160–1) and the ways the Nivkh ceremony linked clans (1999,181–2).

3 Photos of the 1992 ceremonies are in Doeker-Mach 1993, 100–5. Historic photos of Nivkh bear ceremonies on Sakhalin are in Shternberg 1999: 135, 137.

4 Duvan is emphasizing the fact that the links have actually been carved from a single piece of wood in such a way that they move independently, instead of simply being engraved on a flat piece of wood. This technique requires considerable skill.

5 These streamers are made by shaving wood and are often used for cleansing in ceremonies.

6 The instrument is called *udyadyupu*. The rhythms played include "stopping at the lake" and "resting at the mountain pass," which represent stages on the bear's journey back to the land of the taiga people (Smolyak 1996, 125).

7 Chapter 1 and 6, where Belye climbs the ice mountain, protected by her embroidery, and chapter 6, where Yegdyga brings his seal wife back to life.

8 Chapter 4, where the heroine has to contend with the spirit creature who is half man and half dog.

9 Rosugbu 1997.

10 Most of the people I have met who have been healed by Siberian shamans describe the experience of feeling the soul return through the top of the head.

11 Smolyak, Anna, personal communication 1999.

12 I'm not certain why she used the term Gilyak, the name the Nivkh people were known by before the Soviet period. We later confirmed that her mother was Yakut (Sakha) and her father Ul'chi.

13 Anga refers here to their own spirits, not the Christian God.

CHAPTER EIGHT

1 See appendix one for further details.

2 This is not the Christian God but the highest of the Nanai pantheon, Sangi Mapa, with his wife, Sangi Mama. They live on the ninth layer of heaven (Smolyak 1999, 222).

3 In his study of the Chukchi, Waldemar Bogoras writes that if a person found a tiny drum made from the skin of a beetle or even a louse in the tundra, it would give him/her immense shamanic power (Bogoras 1975, 426).

4 In Anna Khodzher's version, the great hunter Ka catches the fox and skins her but she resurrects herself by singing shamanically to the elements.

5 Some say that the dragon is an image imported to the Amur region from China, but local people insist that the dragon has always been part of their pantheon. He seems to act as a heavenly balance to the image of the earthly or lower worldly snake.

6 This story is similar to Valentina Kyalundzyuga's tale of the "Six Brothers and the Squirrels," chapter 6.

7 This is the same reason that the servant woman gives in "The Seagull," chapter 1.

8 There the shaman's bone turns into a woman shaman who defeats his enemies (chapter 5).

9 See chapter 6.

10 I have also heard these words used in storytelling with a different meaning – there ka-ka was used to scare away evil spirits

who might catch the story and through it bring evil into the lives of the listeners.

11 Sometimes the ceremony involves accompanying the soul to *Buni*, sometimes the soul is merely seen off, depending on what the individual needs.

12 E. Gaer describes what may be the same event, adding that the dead man's brother told him that they had killed the wife. She tells of another man who refused to be seen off until his relatives returned an axe he had borrowed to its owner (Gaer 1988, 9).

APPENDICES

1 Some of the Turkic people also continued to move. While the Sayan mountains are considered to be their homeland, Turkic peoples carried their languages and culture ass far west as Turkey and northeastward into eastern Siberia to what is today the Sakha Republic, which extends beyond the Arctic Circle.

2 Personal communication to author.

References and Suggestions
for Further Reading

Aprahamian, S., and K. Kailo, eds. Forthcoming. *The Unbearable Gaze: Wo/men and bears – Transgressing Nature/Culture.* Halifax: Fernwood Publications

Austerlitz, R. 1978. "Folklore, Nationality and the Twentieth Century in Siberia and the Soviet Far East." In Oinas, F.J., ed., *Folklore, Nationalism and Politics.* Columbus, Ohio: Slavica Publications

Avrorin, V.A. 1986. *Materialy po nanaiskomu yazyku i fol'kloru. [Materials on Nanai Language and Folklore.]* Leningrad: Nauka

Balzer, M.M., ed. 1997. *Shamanic Worlds: Rituals and Lore of Siberia and Central Asia.* Armonk, New York: M.E. Sharpe

Basilov, V.N. 1984 a. *Izbranniki Dukhov. [Chosen by the Spirits]* Moscow: Izdatel'stvo politicheskoi literaturoi

Black, Lydia 1973. "The Nivkh (Gilyak) of Sakhalin and the Lower Amur." *Arctic Anthropology* 10, (1): 1–110

– 1988. "Peoples of the Amur and Maritime Regions." In Fitzhugh,

William W., and Aron Crowell, eds., *Crossroads of Continents.*
Washington, D.C.: Smithsonian Institution Press

Bogoras, Waldemar. 1975. *The Chukchi.* Jesup North Pacific
Expedition 7, memoir collection of the American Museum of
Natural History. New York: AMS Press

Campbell, Joseph. 1988. *Historical Atlas of World Mythology.* vol. 1 *The
Way of the Animal Powers.* 147–55. New York: Harper and Row

Comrie, Bernard. 1981. *The Languages of the Soviet Union.*
Cambridge: Cambridge University Press

Dioszegi, V. 1968a. *Popular Beliefs and Folklore Traditions in Siberia.*
Bloomington: Indiana University Press

— 1968b. *Tracing Shamans in Siberia: The Story of an Ethnographical
Research Expedition.* Oosterhout: Anthropological Publications

Dioszegi, V., and M. Hoppál, eds. 1978. *Shamanism in Siberia.*
Budapest: Akademiai Kiado

Doeker-Mach, Günther, 1993. *The Forgotten Peoples of Siberia.* Zürich:
Scalo

Eliade, Mircea. 1964. *Shamanism: An Archaic Technique of Ecstasy.* New
York: Pantheon

Fitzhugh, William W., and Aron Crowell, eds. 1988. *Crossroads of
Continents.* Washington, D.C.: Smithsonian Institution Press

Forsyth, James. 1992. *A History of the Peoples of Siberia.* Cambridge:
Cambridge University Press

Gaer, E.A. 1988. "The Passing Away of the Deceased Man's Soul into
the Next World – Buni." Moscow: Nauka (Central Department of
Oriental Literature) [in English]

— 1991. *Drevnye bytovye obryady nanaitsev [Ancient Everyday Rituals of
the Nanai]* Khabarovsk: Khabarovsk Book Publishers

Grant, Bruce. 1995. *In the Soviet House of Culture.* Princeton, N.J.:
Princeton University Press

Halifax, Joan. 1982. *Shaman, the Wounded Healer.* London: Thames
and Hudson

Hallowell, A. Irving. 1928. "Bear Ceremonialism in the Northern
Hemisphere." American Anthropologist 28: 1–175

Hatto, A.T. 1970. *Shamanism and Epic Poetry in Northern Asia.*
London: University of London

Hoppál, M., ed. 1984. *Shamanism in Eurasia.* Gottingen: Herodot

Humphrey, Caroline. 1980. "Theories of North Asian Shamanism" In Gellner, E., ed., *Soviet and Western Anthropology*. New York: Columbia University Press

Humphrey, Caroline, and Uruge Onon. 1996. *Shamans and Elders*. Oxford: Oxford University Press

Kendall, Laurel. 1988. *The Life and Hard Times of a Korean Shaman*. Honolulu: University of Hawaii Press

– 1987. *Shamans, Housewives, and Other Restless Spirits*. Honolulu: University of Hawaii Press

Kenin-Lopsan, Mongush. 1997. "Tuvan Shamanic Folklore." In Balzer, 1997, 110–52.

Khodzher, Anna Petrovna. 1990. *Duchenku Poet*. Khabarovsk: Khabarovsk Book Publishers

– 1998. *Fox Mischief*. Vancouver: Udagan Books

Kimonko, Jansi. 1985. *Tam, gde bezhit Sukpai [Where the Sukpai Runs]*. Khabarovsk: Khabarovsk Book Publishers

Krushanova, A.I. 1989. *Istorya i kultura Udegeitsev [History and Culture of the Udegei]*. Leningrad: Nauka

Kyalundzyuga, Valentina. 1974. *Dva solntse [Two Suns]* Khabarovsk: Khabarovsk Book Publishers

– 1998. The Ice Mountain. Vancouver B.C: Udagan Books

Laufer, Berthold. 1975. *The Decorative Art of the Amur Tribes*. New York: AMS Press.

Leisiö, Timo. 1999. "The Eurasian Problem of the Octosyllabic Metric Pattern." Presentation at the conference "Shamans – Epics and Ecology." Tampere, Finland

Nagishkin, Dmitrii. 1980. *Amurskie Skazki. [Tales of the Amur]*. Khabarovsk: Khabarovsk Book Publishers

Nicholson, Shirley. 1987. *Shamanism*. Wheaton, Ill. Theosophical Publication House

Novik, Elena S. 1984. *Obryad i fol'klor v sibirskom shamanizme [Rite and Folklore in Siberian Shamanism]*. Moscow: Nauka

– 1997. "The Archaic Epic and Its Relationship to Ritual." In Balzer, 1997, 185–234.

Nowak, M., and S. Durrant. 1977. *The Tale of the Nišan Shamaness*. Seattle: University of Washington Press

Oinas, Felix J. 1978. "The Political Uses and Themes of Folklore in the Soviet Union." In Oinas, F.J. ed., *Folklore, Nationalism, and Politics*. Columbus, Ohio: Slavica Publications

Okladnikov, Alexei. 1981. *Ancient Art of the Amur Region*. Leningrad: Aurora Art Publishers

Ostrovskii, A.B. 1997. *Mifologia i verovania Nivkhov. [Mythology and Beliefs of the Nivkh]*. St Petersburg: Peterburgskoe Vostokovedenie

Podmaskin, V.V. 1991. *Dukhovnaya kul'tura udegeitsev XIX-XXvv. [Spiritual Culture of the Udegei in the XIX- XX c.]*. Vladivostok: Izdatel'stvo dal'nevostochnogo universiteta

Rosugbu, I. 1997. The Semantics of the Ul'chi Toy Doll. Unpublished manuscript

Sangi, Vladimir. 1967. *Legendi ykh-mifa.[Legends of Ykh-mif]*. Moscow: Sovietskaia Rossia

– 1989. *Pesn' o nivkhakh [Song of the Nivkh]*. Moscow: Sovremennik

Shavkunov, E.V. 1968. *Gosudarstvo Bokhai i pamyatniki ego kul'tury v primor'e [The Bokhai State and Monuments of Its Culture in the Primorye]*. Leningrad: Nauka

– 1990. *Kul'tura Chzhurchzhenei-udige [Culture of the Jurchen-udige]*. Moscow: Nauka

Shirokogoroff, S.M. 1935. *Psychomental Complex of the Tungus*. London: Kegan Paul, Trench, Trubner

Shnirel'man, V.A. 1993. *Bikinskie udegeitsy: politika i ekologia [The Bikin Udegei: Policy and Ecology]*. London: Survival International

Shternberg, Lev. 1999. *Social Organization of the Gilyak*. New York and Seattle: American Museum of Natural History and University of Washington Press

Siikala, A.L. 1978. *The Rite-Technique of the Siberian Shaman*. Helsinki: Suomalainen Tiedeakatemia

Simonov, M.D. 1998. *Fol'klor udegeitsev: nimanku, telungu, yekhe [Folklore of the Udegei: Nimanku, telungu and yekhe]. Pamyatniki fol'klora narodov sibiri i dal'nego vostoka [Monuments of Folklore of the Peoples of Siberia and the Far East]*. Novosibirsk: Nauka

Slezkine, Yuri. 1994. *Arctic Mirrors: Russia and the Small Peoples of the North*. Ithaca: Cornell University Press

Slezkine, Yuri, and G. Diment. 1993. *Between Heaven and Hell*. New York: St Martin's Press

Smolyak, Anna. 1991. *Shaman: lichnost', funktsii, mirovozzrenie*

[Shaman: Personality, Function and Worldview]. Moscow: Nauka
— 1995. "Dva obryada kasa" ["Two *kasa* rituals"]. In Funk, D.A. ed., *Shamanizm i rannie religioznye predstavlenia [Shamanism and Early Religious Concepts]*. Moscow: Russian Academy of Sciences
— 1996. *Ul'chi: Khozyaistvo, kul'tura i byt v proshlom i nastoyashchem [The Ulchi: Economy, Culture, and Way of Life in the Past and Present]*. Moscow: Nauka
Vahtre, Lauri, and Jüri Viikberg. *Red Book of the Peoples of the Russian Empire.* http://julia.eki.ee/books/redbook/
Vakhtin, Nikolai. 1994. "Native Peoples of the Russian Far North." In Minority Rights Group, ed., *Polar Peoples: Self Determination and Development.* London: Minority Rights Publications
Van Deusen, Kira. 1996a. "The Flying Tiger: Aboriginal Women Shamans, Storytellers, and Embroidery Artists in the Russian Far East." *Shaman* (1-2): 45–78
— 1996b. "Protection and Empowerment: Clothing Symbolism in the Amur River Region of the Russian Far East." In Buys, Cunera, and Jarich Oosten, eds., *Braving the Cold: Continuity and Change in Arctic Clothing.* Leiden: National Museum of Ethnology
— 1997. "Ul'chi Shamans." *Shaman* 5 (2): 155–64
— 1999a. "Women's Stories among Indigenous Peoples of the Russian Far East." In MacDonald, M.R., ed. *Traditional Storytelling Today.* London and Chicago: Fitzroy-Dearborn
— 1999b. "Storytelling as a Shamanic Art: The Udegei People of the Amur Region." In Funk, D.A., and V.I. Kharitonova, eds., *Shamanism and Other Indigenous Beliefs and Practices,* 96–104. Moscow: Russian Academy of Sciences
— 1999c. *Raven and the Rock: Storytelling in Chukotka.* Seattle: University of Washington Press and Canadian Circumpolar Institute
Vitebsky, Piers. 1996. *Shaman: An Illustrated Guide (Living Wisdom).* New York: Little Brown

Index

accompanying souls of dead. *See* shamanic ceremonies

Achan, 217-22

Adikhini, 119–22

Ainu, 152, 229

Alfred, Jerry, 60

alphabets, 17, 187, 233, 241n4. *See also* writing systems

amba, 53, 113, 221. *See also* spirits, evil

amulets, 83, 88, 124

Amur River, *149*, 227; pollution, 72

Amursk, 215–17

ancestral figures, 19. *See also* spirits, figures; *sevén*

ancestry: human, 20; shamanic, xiii; of Udegei people, 49

Anga, xxv, 166–74 163, *167*

applique, 28, *59, 75, 78, 104, 162, 167, 179, 218*

archaeology, 94, 191

Arseniev, V.K., 35, 49

Audubon Society, 3

Baikal-Amur mainline, 191

Balzer, M., 238, 239

Basilov, V., 238

bear: ceremony, 23, 67, 152–5, 153, 245n3, 6; dull-witted, 197–8, 204–6; helper, 45–8; hunting, 23, 67, 122; marriage with, 23–5, 39; transformation to, 67; and twins, 67

Beldi, Galya, 71

Beldi, Leonid Maktuvich, 71–4, 72

Beldi, Maria Antonovna, 219–22

Beldi, Maria Grigorievna, 74–9

Beldi, Nikolai Petrovich, 108–12

Beldi, Nina, 71

Beldi, Olga, 75

Beldi, Olga Grigorievna, 97

belt. *See yampa*

Belye, 11, 82

bioenergetics, 244ch4n4

birchbark, 33, 92–3

bird, as symbol of soul, 123–4, 243n6

birth: magic, 18; miraculous, 63

blood, healing power of, 106

boats, 18, 34

Bogoras, Waldemar, 243n7, 246n3

Bohai State, 229

bones, 12–14, 39, 48, 51, 111, 154, 201–3, 211–12

Books, burning of, 187, 234

breath, 162

Bulava, 148–84

Buni, 122. *See also* shamanic ceremonies, accompanying the dead

burning: animal skin, 102; books, 187, 234; evil spirits, 54, 88

cannibals, 13, 138–40

Christianity, 60–2, 110, 231, 243n4

clans, 25, 187–8, 228–9, 231–2

climate, 125, 217, 228

clothing, 26–9. *See also* applique; embroidery

collectivization of labour, 233

comb, 12, 16, 84, 85

communism and traditional beliefs, 110

consciousness, altered states, 67, 69, 122

constellations, 136

creation, of earth, 17, 20, 138–40

crocodiles, 125–6, 216–17, 228

Dada, 71–93

dairy farming, 72

death and rebirth, 17, 32, 96, 111–12

Dechuli, Mado, 150–1

deities, 32, 246n2

Dersu Usala, 35

Digor, Ksenia, 207–15, *209*

Dioszegi, V., 239

disobedience, 89

divination, 17, 125, 128, 155, 166

dog: as evil spirit, 82–7; as helper, 51; as protagonist, 105–8

dolls, 161

dragon, *194*–5, 207, 246n5

dreams, 11, 97, 111, 112

drum, 114, 120, 122, 126, 169,

190, 244ch6n1
violin, Nanai, 90–3. *See also*
  musical instruments
Vitebsky, P. 237
vodka, 55, 169, 219
volcano, 18–20

water of life, 32–3
wealth, 245n11
weather station, 119
"Who Is the Strongest?" 102–3
Where the Eagle Flies, 239
wife. *See* spouse
Wind, Master of, 29–31, 142–7
women: abuse of, 78, 97, 105,
  233; as shamans, xvi; social
  position, 225, 231–3. *See also*
  storytellers, women as
woodcarving, *164–5*
World War II, 65
writing systems, 62

yampa, 22, 114, 120, *129*, 169,
  185, 219
yasak (tribute), 243n4
Ycha, Ymynda, 151–3, 155–8
Yegdyga, 11, 82
ypila (prayer), 219
Yukon International Storytelling
  Festival, 3, 20